Table of Contents:

Table of Contents cont:

Dedications:

This book is dedicated to all those who God has bestowed specific information upon and felt compelled to disseminate it for the advancement of humanity. God speaks in signs. We interpret the signs. Hopefully, humanity is advanced.

I also dedicate this work to my future self. The Dalai Lama has it right, he leaves his material possessions to himself after his death. I leave this information to my future reincarnated 'selves', so they too can know a realistic and practical use for Stonehenge, other than for sun and moon alignments.

Lastly, I dedicate the information contained in this book to the pursuit of ideas. Ideas have the best chance at becoming eternal and transcending time. Everything else breaks down, deteriorates, erodes, rusts, dies, bankrupts, supersedes, explodes, or implodes. They are also the uniting element of humanity. Can we all agree to disagree, and not kill each other over ideas? Allow yourself the humility to be wrong without forcing what you perceive as 'right' onto others. I hope my thoughts and ideas regarding the site, structure, cosmology, and our ancestors stand the test of time.

God bless humanity and our ideas.

Concept of the Book:

My second intent for this book was to get across the ideas and discoveries, so to interest young people and fan their enthusiasm for discovery. The prose and language of the writing is intended for a younger audience. Adults can read down, but it is hard for children to read up. I also did not go too deeply into some issues for fear of presenting wrong information and going beyond my knowledge. I hope the reader is interested enough to continue the research to its final conclusion. In no way did I cover all the hidden aspects of Stonehenge. Allow this work to be a springboard because after 5,000 years, please do not mothball Stonehenge.

Also, as an architect, I considered the ADA regulations. I purposely provided larger than normal font size for older adult reading, as well as, my own. The layout of the book also has architectural influences with regard to page numbering and naming of the diagrams. I also attempted to be as transparent as possible with regard to my thinking, research, development, and conclusions. As an architect, my duty is to the life, safety, and welfare of my community. I place this work somewhere between the 'life' and 'welfare' of my reader.

The Riders discussed at the rear of the book are information and ideas I have held onto for a very long time. I felt it all needed to be sent out to the four corners of the compass rose, in order to see where it can grow.

Finally, a plea to English Heritage who governs the site, please return it back to its original function by allowing cremated remains to be buried there. I'm sure there is a spot that would not affect its historical value. It should not remain a ship in a corked bottle. Please, open the bottle, and let's all say cheers!

Acknowledgments:

Thanks to God, most of all. The spiritual gas of this endeavor came at a pivotal point in my life and a turning point in my career. Studying and pursuing the lost knowledge of Stonehenge propelled me through a turbulent period in my life. Focusing on it maintained my sanity and esteem. I offer the same advice to all those readers who are, or may enter, a pivotal period in their life. Grab on to something challenging and bigger than yourself. Hold on until it sees you through. It's true that another day makes all the difference in the world.

Thanks also to Gary Carolan and Richard Meyer of Goodwin Funeral Home and Cremation Services. They employed me when I needed work and offered flexible hours, so I could pursue writing. They also have been supportive friends. It's wonderful to watch experts at their craft. They are impeccable with their clients; dedicated, professional, understanding, caring, and knowledgeable with both the bereaved and the deceased. Their contact information is: www.goodwinfh.com (603) 625-5703.

An important, "thanks much" must go out to Thomas Weber, who helped me get through architecture school. Without him, it just would not have been any fun. Also, for joining me in my quest to Stonehenge, driving me all around England when I did not have the guts to drive myself, and for being my lifetime brick. "Chug and run".

Thanks to my wife Marjorie, who suffered through my tunnel vision for several years while researching and writing this book. I rank her up with Noah's wife. She too had to suffer through her husband's endeavor.

Finally, I have to thank all those who received my resume and ignored it, and those who interviewed me and did not hire me. It left me open to other possibilities.

Introduction: Chapter 1

Reader's Notes

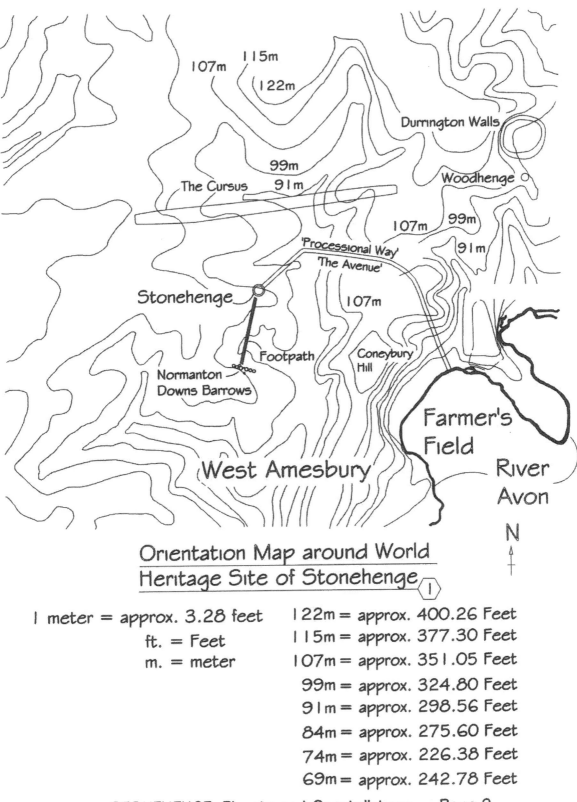

107m 115m
122m

Durrington Walls

The Cursus 99m 91m

Woodhenge

107m 99m

91m

'Processional Way'
'The Avenue'

Stonehenge

107m

Footpath Coneybury
Hill

Normanton
Downs Barrows

Farmer's
Field

West Amesbury

River
Avon

N

Orientation Map around World
Heritage Site of Stonehenge ⬡1

1 meter = approx. 3.28 feet   122m = approx. 400.26 Feet
ft. = Feet   115m = approx. 377.30 Feet
m. = meter   107m = approx. 351.05 Feet
                                99m = approx. 324.80 Feet
                                91m = approx. 298.56 Feet
                                84m = approx. 275.60 Feet
                                74m = approx. 226.38 Feet
                                69m = approx. 242.78 Feet

STONEHENGE: Planets and Constellations.....Page 2

My interest in researching Stonehenge was unforeseen and the discoveries detailed in this body of work, I can only assume, were intended for me to reveal to the public. I leave the importance and benefits of these findings to the reader and academic community. I assure everyone that the discoveries discussed here have not been twisted or falsified in any way in order to support a result.

Foremost, while examining and investigating Stonehenge, I wore the hat of an Architect with the mind-set of a critical thinker; constantly asking the structure and site, "why", "what for", "to what end", and "for what purpose"? Then, figuratively speaking, I let the site speak to me. From this, I acquired the ears to listen. It was as if I emptied my cup of all preconceived ideas and mysticism regarding the site, and allowed myself to become the student.

To me, every element of the site had at least one purpose and a reason for being. No element, not even the smallest detail, was seen as being haphazard, whimsical, or frivolous. Also, my strategy was to develop a hypothesis, then determine if it was valid, in lieu of forcing a purpose or reason onto any particular element, in order to substantiate a conclusion.

The site we see and are able to visit today is the culmination of approximately 5,000 years of design intent, consisting of construction, renovation, and destruction. Peeling back and dating the historic onion of Stonehenge can be daunting. Per my research, there is not a clear consensus in archaeology on the number of phases it has experienced, but with advancements in technology, estimated time frames for construction have been accepted. However, I disagree with the term 'phases' so commonly associated with this site because, as an architect, it implies that there was a single generation of builders on this site handing down knowledge and design intent to their kin folk. It may have happened that way, but I take exception to the implication. I prefer to consider the onion of Stonehenge as sequential 'eras'. An era of people developing its initial intent; eras of people adding to and modifying the site for their own purpose and use; eras of people investigating and speculating what and how the site was used.

The general accepted starting date of the site, beginning with the construction of an inner and an outer ring of earthen-mounds separated by a huge ditch, is approximately 3,000 to 2,900 BCE.⟨1⟩ But, giving myself artistic license, I set the date on May 19, 3018 BCE since it has an interesting astronomical correlation with the planet Mars.*⟨2⟩

Attempting to understand the details of the site, while at the same time broadening my knowledge of astronomy, I asked myself a poignant question, "What would I need to have in order to get familiar with astronomy, if I lived 5,000 years ago"? I believe the answer was the same for them as it was for me in 2015 CE. We both needed a consistent plain from which to view celestial bodies and a consistent manner in which to gauge time.

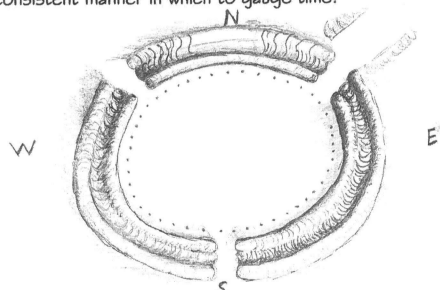

Learning that the inner bank of the mounds may have been constructed to a height between 5 to 6 feet and that they may not have been maintained for a lengthy period of time after completion, led me to ask another question, "What could the mounds have been used for that would have given them a temporary purpose"?

*See ref. note #2;

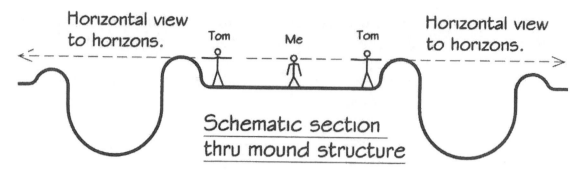

Horizontal view to horizons.

Tom   Me   Tom

Horizontal view to horizons.

Schematic section thru mound structure

The architectural profession uses 5 1/2 feet as a typical viewing height. It made sense to me that they too would have needed to see the planets and stars appear and disappear from a consistent eye level perspective. But, I had to visit the site in order to experience reality. With the assistance of my friend Tom Weber, we were able to gauge the visual height of the existing horizons by Tom extending his arms horizontal from his sides. As I stood a distance away from him, I could not see the horizons. This told me that a mound 5 1/2 feet tall would have been high enough to provide a false backdrop, from which to view celestial bodies.

Our early ancestors were occupying lands with the present day national borders of Britain, Ireland, Scotland, France, and Spain, for thousands of years prior to 3000 BCE. In these areas there are many examples of cave art, mounds, mortuary structures, standing stones, post holes, domesticated animal bones, human remains, tools, flints, pottery, and the like. They learned and used the sky, with all its celestial bodies, both during the day and at night; for time keeping, travel, religious worship, planting, harvesting, and funeral proceedings.

The genesis of my initial investigation of the site was to further understand the reason behind the placement of 56 cavities [13] lining the inner perimeter of the mounds. Many of the cavities have been excavated and were found to contain cremated human remains. For a very long time the cavities have been an unassuming element on the site compared to that of the standing ring of towering stones. So, it goes to show how critical thinking and small details can translate into grand discoveries. The curiosity that fueled my interest was not directed at their use, which to me was obvious, but at their number, symmetry, and geometry. Why were 56 cavities constructed, why were they equally spaced, and why were they set in a circle?

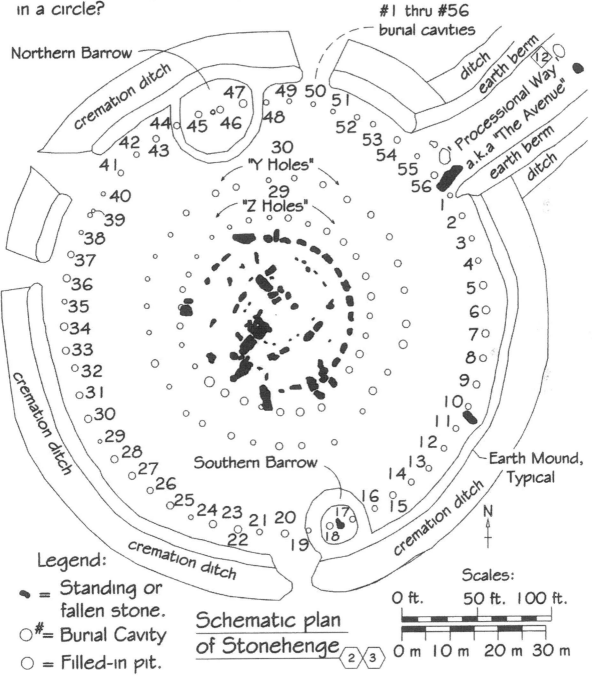

Schematic plan of Stonehenge

Legend:
- ◖ = Standing or fallen stone.
- ○# = Burial Cavity
- ○ = Filled-in pit.

Scales:
0 ft. 50 ft. 100 ft.
0 m 10 m 20 m 30 m

STONEHENGE: Planets and Constellations.....Page 6

Our ancestors were experts at astronomy, much better than the average person on any city street corner today. We look at a watch or phone to determine the hour and date. Our ancestors used the day and night sky for determining time, thus one of the great needs for Stonehenge.

At a minimum, it became their observatory, clock, calendar, church, hospital, funeral home, and cemetery. In essence, it was an overall civic structure built to last many generations and celestial occurrences. No written historical records have been found regarding the people and how the structure was used. I can only surmise its purpose based on the details of my discoveries while comparing them to other historical sites predating Stonehenge.

The early cultures of Sumer, Babylon, and the Pre-dynastic Period of Egypt were located in communities adjacent the Mediterranean Sea. Each of these communities predated Stonehenge and each provided historical written records describing their culture and religious beliefs. It was from these areas where early advancements in technology, agriculture, writing, astronomy, mathematics, commerce, and farming developed and spread; reaching the Atlantic coast of Europe by 5,000 BCE.◇③

Throughout history, it has been determined that when people met while trading, they shared ideas and technologies among each other. The region of present day Spain and France have shorelines that abut both the Mediterranean Sea and the Atlantic Ocean. This would have been a wonderful land bridge to the waters of the English Channel. They would have built a boat and migrated to England for resources, trade, and prosperity.

Schematic plan of Africa, Britan, Europe, and Middle East

It is very plausible that influential people crossed the English Channel and communicated with the existing inhabitants, or stayed and became part of the community. Agriculture and farming is said to have begun in Britain by 4000 BCE,◇ approximately 1,000 years before the mounds of Stonehenge were constructed.

Building on the knowledge and discoveries of our ancestors, we now take for granted the earth is a sphere, spinning counterclockwise on a tilted axis while rotating around the sun. We also take for granted the naming and charting of the celestial stars that make up the constellations. The name, shape, character, and legend of each of the constellations has changed over time. Throughout history, each civilization has developed their own story surrounding them. To help confuse matters, civilizations would borrow and adopt constellations from each other, adapting them to their culture, needs, and individual purpose.

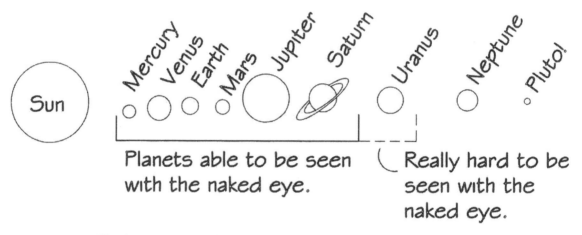

Planets able to be seen with the naked eye.

Really hard to be seen with the naked eye.

Schematic elevation of our solar system

There have been times in human history where parts of this information was discovered and then lost, only to be rediscovered centuries later, by other observers.

The historical knowledge gathered and destroyed in the burning of the Library of Alexandria, is a prime example of this. The culmination of ancestral intelligence and ancient technology was forever lost. Important information concerning the knowledge of Stonehenge, along with its construction, may have been included among the documents lost in that fire.

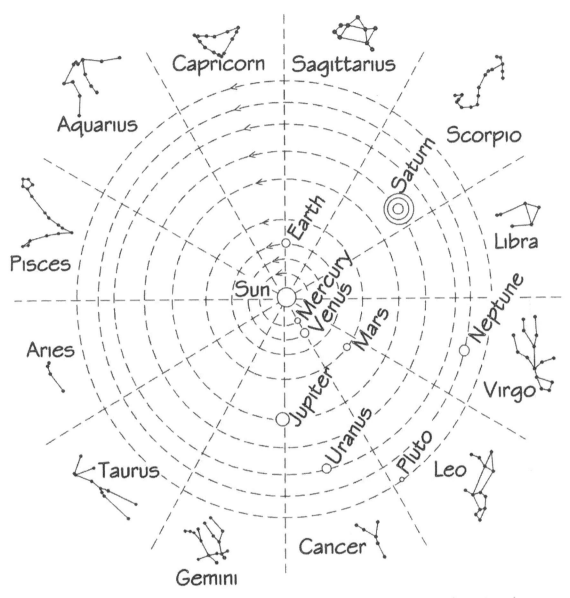

Schematic constellation and planets in quadrant plan

Quite possibly, it is now being rediscovered due to my research, and by those who use the ideas presented in this document. For example, Copernicus, who conducted his research in the 1540's CE, is recognized as discovering the sun, not the earth, is at the center of our solar system with all the other planets moving around it.

Prior to Copernicus, a man named Aristarchus of Samos, who lived as a Greek astronomer and mathematician about 230 BCE, was the first known person to produce an accurate model of our solar system with the sun at the center. In the fields of astronomy, mathematics, medicine, weaponry, architecture, etc., modern researchers have discovered that, in many instances, we have been playing a game of catch-up; merely rediscovering technologies thought invented in our modern era.

The Sumerian culture, which existed about 4000 BCE, had a very meaningful impact on history, as we know it today. It is known, through their cuneiform writings, that they were aware of at least 11 celestial bodies that make up our solar system: our Sun, Mercury, Venus, Earth, our Moon, Mars, Saturn, Jupiter, Uranus, Neptune, and Pluto. The Sun through to Uranus can be seen with the naked eye. A profound invention, which we still use today, was their arithmetic. They based their numbering system on the unit 10 and then multiplied by 6 to get the next unit, such as, 60. The advantage of their system and the reason it was adopted by other cultures, is because the unit numbers are very divisible by other numbers. For example, the number 60 is divisible by: 60, 30, 20, 15, 12, 10, 6, 5, 4, 3, 2, and 1. They also get credit for dividing the circumference of a circle into 360 degrees and dividing the units of the day into hours, minutes, and seconds.⟨5⟩

How the Sumerians knew of Neptune and Pluto without the use of a telescope is not relevant, but what is relevant and important to express, is the fact that a pre-existing culture had knowledge of the planets in their proper order and a counting system for which to interact with the world around them. It is also relevant to state that some historians say Sumerians had knowledge the planets orbited around the sun thousands of years before it was discovered by Aristarchus of Samos, and then again by Copernicus. Stonehenge may be the evidence that historians need for proving that early ancestors were knowledgeable people and how information is easily lost.

The 56 cavities of Mars: Chapter 2

My interpretation of the site is: The builders had knowledge of Mars, were tracking its position in the night sky, calculated the number of days in its orbital cycle around the sun while they compared it to earth's. I realize this is a profound and bold statement, but for me, clarity came with my discovery that 56 are to Mars, as 30 are to Earth.

It takes Earth approximately 365.25 and Mars approximately 686.9 days to orbit once around the sun. My eureka moment was making the connection between the equally spaced circular pattern of the 56 burial cavities located around the perimeter of the site and dividing them into the number of days in a Martian orbital cycle, whereby receiving an answer of approximately 12.26 days. Comparing that answer to the number of days in Earth's orbital cycle, divided by 30 (one month) and receiving a similar answer of approximately 12.16 days. The two answers are almost identical and too coincidental not to have been investigated further.

The difference between the two answers is about 5.6 days during one Martian orbital cycle around the sun. 12.26 days - 12.16 days = .1 day; .1 x 56 = 5.6 days.

$$12.26 \text{ days} \longleftrightarrow 12.16 \text{ days}$$

$$56 \overline{)686.9} \text{ days} \qquad 30 \overline{)365.25} \text{ days}$$

To me, what makes this connection even more profound, spiritual, and God inspired is the fact that I did not know the number of days in a Martian orbital cycle prior to tasking myself to make the comparison. I was driving on the expressway, mulling over the question of the 56 cavities when the idea of Mars slipped into my consciousness. I began intuitively imagining 56, or even 59, having something to do with Mars. To me, this could have been a moment of a 'past-life blur', meaning that one of my past life experiences was revealing itself in the present moment.

Additional clues that the 56 cavities were used as 12.16-day planetary markers symbolizing the path of Mars through the solar system, reside in their general description by archaeologists. They have been described as being very equally spaced within an accurate 288 feet diameter circle. Each location consists of a hole where the sides are very steep and the bottom is flat, ranging between 2 to 4 feet in depth.⟨6⟩ Researchers have confirmed that 23 of the 36 cavities excavated contain cremated human remains. In addition, many of those were re-opened several times in order to add additional remains⟨7⟩ In essence, the cavities are burial crypts. In additon, vast areas of the ditches surrounding the outside of the mound enclosure, also contain cremated remains. The site is a cemetery.⟨7⟩

The comparison lies in the knowledge the 56 cavities are 144 feet from the center of the site and Mars has an average distance of approximately 142 million miles from the sun. I highlight this information because there are also 30 holes ringing the outside of the stone structure that are approximately 90 feet from the center of the site. Earth's average distance from the sun is approximately 93 million miles. I believe the 30 holes, which are known as the 'Y Holes', represent the elliptical orbit of earth and the 56 cavities represent the orbit of Mars.

I am not implying that each foot is equal to a million miles, but I am implying that there are proportional ratios at play on this site, and at some period in Stonehenge's construction, the users were using the site as a planetary chart; experimenting with both circular and elliptical orbits designed to help explain and predict planetary movement around the sun.

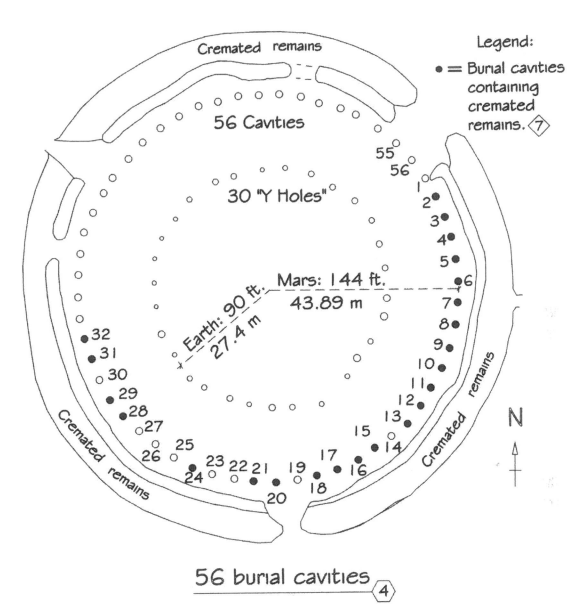

Cremated remains

56 Cavities

30 "Y Holes"

Legend:
• = Burial cavities containing cremated remains. ⟨7⟩

55
56
1
2•
3•
4•
5•
6
7
8
9
10
11
12
13
14
15
16
17
18
19
20
21
22
23
24
25
26
27
28•
29•
30
31•
32•

Mars: 144 ft.
43.89 m

Earth: 90 ft.
27.4 m

Cremated remains

Cremated remains

N

56 burial cavities ⟨4⟩

The Martian orbit is elliptical; this we know due to Johannes Kepler's research and mathematical computations in the 1600's CE. His discovery was the first written confirmation of planets having elliptical orbits. Until Kepler, the orbits of the planets were thought to be circular. Furthermore, historians believe that earth's position around the sun began being determined 2,250 years ago with the Hellenistic viewpoints from thinkers and observers such as Eratosthenes, Plato, Aristotle, Epicurus, and Ptolemy. I believe

Stonehenge is proof that it all began much earlier than previously expected, about 2,300 years earlier, and with much greater accuracy.

There have been many proportioning systems derived throughout history to bring unity and order to the built environment, I believe the builders of Stonehenge used 'time' as their organizing system. The diagram shows a straight line between cavities 56 and 16, representing the passage of approximately 194 days (12.16 days x 16 gaps = 194.56 days). Curiously, the line crosses over the 30 "Y holes" representing earth's orbit.

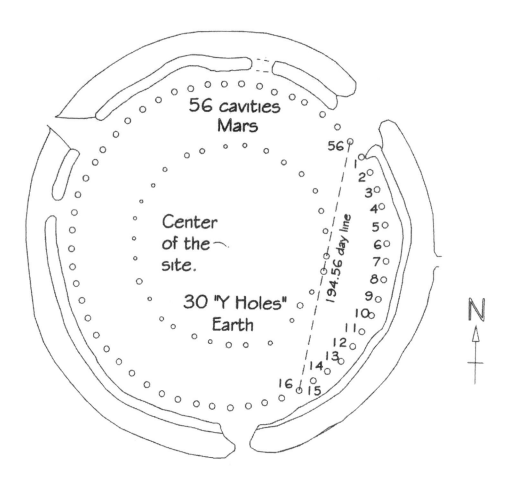

194 days between cavities

I continued checking the consistency of my discovery. Only a few of the 'Y Holes' escaped from being framed in by a 194-day line, which I accounted as a prehistoric experiment of planetary elliptical orbits.

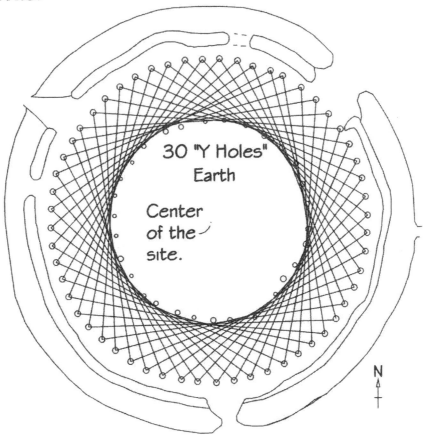

30 "Y Holes"
Earth

Center
of the
site.

N

194 day line frames in Earth's orbit

Remembering that the 'Y Holes' are approximately 90 feet and the 56 cavities are 144 feet from the center, I began performing mathematical, diagrammatic, and proportional relationship investigations among the site elements. To my surprise, I recognized that a 1.88 step-down ratio of time is represented in the built environment of Stonehenge, meaning the divisor of 1.88 remains constant in each equation but the quotient in the beginning equation becomes the dividend in the next, and so on.

$$365 \text{ days} \overline{\smash{\big)}\ 686.9 \text{ days}}^{\ 1.88}$$

365 days	194 days	103 days	55 days	29 days	15.5 days

$$1.88\overline{\smash{\big)}686.9}\text{ days} ; \quad 1.88\overline{\smash{\big)}365}\text{ days} ; \quad 1.88\overline{\smash{\big)}194}\text{ days} ; \quad 1.88\overline{\smash{\big)}103}\text{ days} ; \quad 1.88\overline{\smash{\big)}55}\text{ days} ; \quad 1.88\overline{\smash{\big)}29}\text{ days}$$

I paid particular attention to circumferences, diameters, and radii of site elements to see if I could identify any repeated geometry or mathematical correlation among their size and placement, thus making them purposeful and intentional, in lieu of pure dumb luck.

$2 \cdot \pi \cdot r$ = circumference of a circle. $\pi = 3.1415926\ldots$

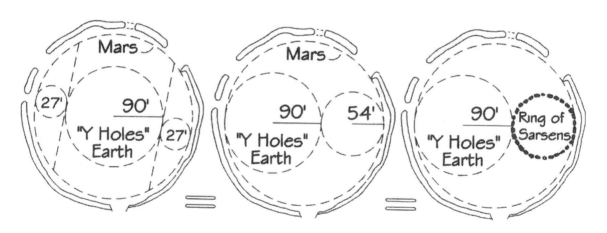

On page 12 of Christopher Chippindale's book, Stonehenge Complete, he provides an inner diameter dimension between the sarsens of 100 feet, and an average sarsen stone width of 3 3/4 feet wide. Adding the diameter of 100 feet and the average width of two sarsen stones together equals about 107 1/2 feet. The diameter of a 54-foot radius circle is 108 feet. To me, there is a proportional system related to the orbital time between Earth and Mars.

What I found to be really interesting is the fact that the proportions of two 194-day circumferences, when added together, equal the proportion of the outside diameter of the sarsen structure.   Also, the proportion of a 365-day circumference, when add to two 194-day circumferences equal the proportion of the circumference of the 686 day circumference. I began to see a proportional 'time machine' at Stonehenge.

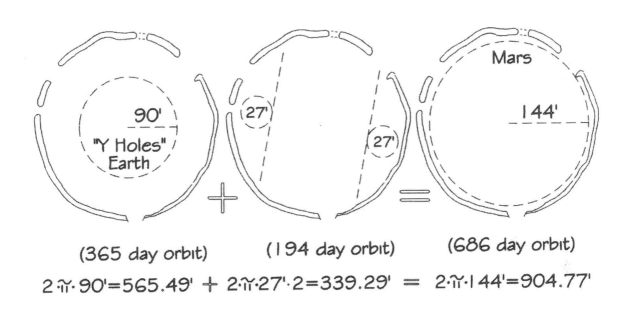

(365 day orbit)   (194 day orbit)   (686 day orbit)

$2 \cdot \Upsilon \cdot 90' = 565.49' + 2 \cdot \Upsilon \cdot 27' \cdot 2 = 339.29' = 2 \cdot \Upsilon \cdot 144' = 904.77'$

According to the step-down proportional ratio, there should be a relationship with the timing of 103 days related to the site. 103 days divided by 12.16 days is equal to 8.47 gaps on the circumference of Mars' orbit. A line drawn from cavity 56 to a location halfway between cavity 8 and 9, creates a circle with a diameter of 16 feet 2 inches wide.   The circumference of the circle representing the orbit of Mars is 904.77 feet, if it is divided 56 times, each gap will be 16.16 or 16' - 2" wide. Per this investigation and discovery, the spacing of the gaps between the cavities was determined by a 1.88 time ratio using Earth and Mars orbital cycles.

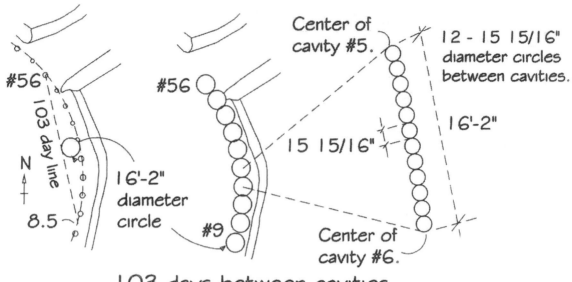

Center of cavity #5.

12 - 15 15/16" diameter circles between cavities.

#56

#56

15 15/16"

16'-2"

N

103 day line

8.5

16'-2" diameter circle

#9

Center of cavity #6.

103 days between cavities

904.778 feet / 56 cavities = 16.156 or 16'-2" between cavities. If the gap between each cavity is equal to the passing of 12.16 days then the distance of each day equals 1.328 feet or 1'-3 15/16" or 15 15/16"; rounded is 16".

Time and distance calculator: 365 days / 12.16 days (12 days 3 hours 50 minutes) = 30 hole locations. 686 days / 12.16 days = 56.41 hole locations. 12.16 x .41 = 4.99 days. This means that the timing between the Mars cavities and the Earth holes are approximately 2.5 days off per year.

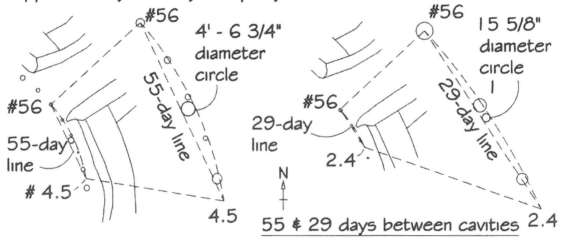

#56

4' - 6 3/4" diameter circle

55-day line

#56

55-day line

4.5

4.5

#56

29-day line

2.4

N

#56

15 5/8" diameter circle

29-day line

2.4

55 & 29 days between cavities

1.88 step-down of days to diameter circle:

686.9 days = 288' - 0" diameter circle
365 days = 180' - 0" diameter circle
194 days = 108' - 0" diameter circle
103 days = 16' - 2" diameter circle
55 days = 4' - 6 3/4" diameter circle
29 days = 1' - 2 5/8" or 15 5/8" diameter circle
15.5 days = 4" diameter circle

Continuing the phenomenon of the step-down proportional ratio, 55 days equates to a diameter of 4 feet 6 3/4 inches, 29 days equates to 15 5/8 inches, and 15.5 days equates to a 4 inch diameter circle. If 16'-2" is divided by 12.16, the answer is 15 15/16 inches, which is extremely similar to 15 5/8 inches. They were able to determine each individual day's movement around the perimeter with great consistency.

Stonehenge was built and organized using these proportional increments. The units of feet are only provided for the reader's sense of scale. They did not use this 12th century invention of measurement, but a standard of proportional measurement, quite possibly, only for this site. Douglas C. Heggie, on page 33 of his book titled Megalithic Science, states that a 'megalithic yard' is equal to about 2.72 feet or 0.829 meters. Half of his megalithic yard is about 16 5/16 inches. There is less than a one-inch difference between a Stonehenge '29-day' increment and half of Heggie's 'megalithic yard'.

There is additional evidence this proportional system had been used to organize other elements on the plan, as well as in elevation. I have included several important examples that I found interesting:

On page 12 of <u>Stonehenge Complete</u>, Chippindale states that the, "flat top (of the lintels) are about 16 feet above the ground".

The thickness of the lintels, to that of the sarsens, are proportional.

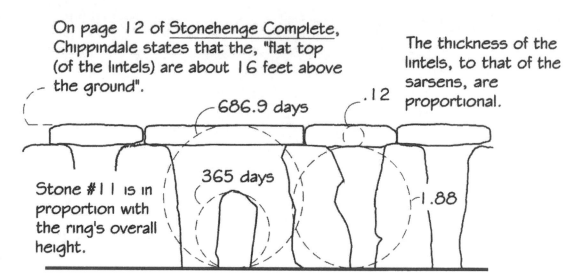

686.9 days

.12

365 days

Stone #11 is in proportion with the ring's overall height.

1.88

Proportional elevation

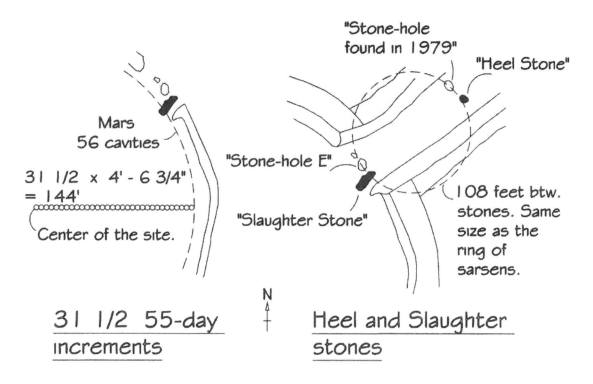

"Stone-hole found in 1979"

"Heel Stone"

Mars
56 cavities

31 1/2 x 4' - 6 3/4" = 144'

Center of the site.

"Stone-hole E"

"Slaughter Stone"

108 feet btw. stones. Same size as the ring of sarsens.

31 1/2 55-day increments

N

Heel and Slaughter stones

The distance of 144 feet from the center of the site to the 56 cavities equals 31 1/2 increments of 4'-6 3/4" and the distance between the Slaughter Stone and Heel Stone is the same size as that of the ring of Sarsens. There also may have been a proportional ratio between the distances of the stones at the base with those at the top.

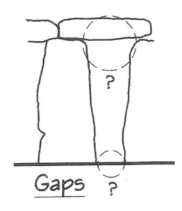

Gaps ?

To help answer how they could have determined an accurate number of days in a Martian orbital cycle, I became familiar with Kepler's research. After reviewing his mathematical calculations, and not understanding them much myself, I concluded that Kepler's computations would have been far too advanced for early civilization; that accuracy and exactness did not play as an important role to our ancestors as it does to us today. I decided to hang my hat on their need for consistency, in lieu of accuracy, with regard to celestial observations.

From my research I discovered that Kepler's predecessors relied on planetary opposition to determine the orbital cycle of Mars. Although, not as exact and accurate as Kepler's computations, this method was a path forward in providing an answer to my question, but in simple terms, what is planetary opposition?

Superior planetary opposition occurs when earth is positioned in-line and between the sun and the outer planets, such as Mars, Jupiter, Saturn, or Uranus. The planets in our solar system orbit around the sun in a counterclockwise direction and all their orbits are relatively flat to each other and relatively on center with the sun.

Learning some of this for the first time while trying to understand how the people of Stonehenge may have used it; rightly or wrongly, common sense dictated to me that opposition of the outer planets would be at the peak of their path through the night sky; south at midnight. This was a good place for me to embark since I like the observational theory of planetary opposition. It is observation, mixed with theory, and just a little bit of simple math. This is something I believe our ancestors would have been able to perform. But now, I had to provide an answer to another imposing question. How were they able to capture time in order to determine the moment of midnight? Being untrained in the art of astronomy, this is something I had to discover for myself.

Midnight at Stonehenge: Chapter 3

The universe, as seen from earth, is in constant flux. The planets and our moon are all in their own orbits. The stars appear to be ever moving since we view them from our own orbiting, tilted, and spinning platform we call earth. It is like watching chocolate chip batter being slowly mixed in a blender. To derive order from the cosmos, an observer must frequently freeze similar moments in time. It would be like taking snapshots of the sky at the same time and same place every night, and then comparing them to each other. Over many instances, the observer would be able to truly distinguish the nightly change in celestial movement from the visual swirl produced from the rotation of the earth.

I chose midnight as my snapshot in time because it is completely opposite the noonday sun and Stonehenge is at such a high latitude, that the evening and morning sun in the summer months can make for very long days. Midnight in this region is a consistently dark period of time; choosing it, allows the influence of the sun's light to completely vanish.

An observer of the solar system is quite able to tell the hours of the day and break the day and night into divisions by observing and utilizing the movements of the sun, moon, and stars; but most especially, in combination with one another. It is also possible and very plausible to use the rhythm of a drum or the beating of a human heart as an instrument of primitive time keeping. It is known that Egyptian ships maintained their oar strokes by beating a drum and it is widely accepted in the medical community that an adult male's heart beats approximately 60 times per minute, while at rest.

In order to determine midnight, they would have had to invent a directional system, something we call a 'compass rose'. Determining the direction of south would have been the easiest component to solve. Observing a shadow cast from any straight stick placed standing in the ground will determine the direction of south, once the sun has reached its highest point in the sky. Such a construction is called a 'gnomon' and a shadow cast from it can indicate the divisions of the day; especially high noon, when the shadow cast is at its shortest in length.

Once south was established, the other three cardinal directions; north, east, and west would have been determined by thinking in terms of equal, opposite, and perpendicular directions. This system of division is fundamental logic and not hard to accept. There is archaeological evidence that the Sumerians developed their own system by dividing the circumference of a circle into 360 equal divisions, called degrees, which we still use today.

After the four cardinal points were determined, they could have been subdivided into many smaller units. The number of times a circle can be divided is limitless, but the divisions get pretty crowded if subdivided much more than 360 times. When the 'compass rose' was completed, the user could gauge the passing of objects in the sky to determine midnight.

Compass Rose:
Courtesy of Pete Knese

STONEHENGE: Planets and Constellations.....Page 24

Beginning at noon and tracking the sun's position to the following noon, the earth rotates 360 degrees. 360 degrees divided by 24 hours is 15 degrees per hour. The builders of Stonehenge may also have divided their day into 56 units in lieu of 24. If they did then each unit would have been about 25 1/2 minutes long compared to our standard unit of 60 minutes.

Critical for interpreting midnight is understanding or assuming the sun is on the opposite side of the earth half-a-day after high noon, thus indicating midnight at Stonehenge.

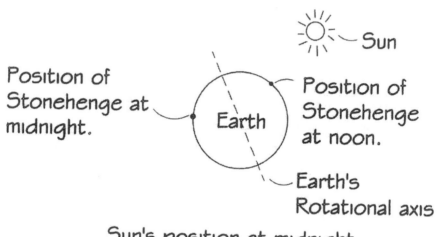

Sun's position at midnight

As an example, if an observer watches the sun disappear at dusk over the cavity marked #31 on the plan on the next page, the time of day would be, 11 points and 11 gaps past noon. Midnight would occur with the passing of 17 more points and gaps. Critical for consistency in timekeeping is bridging the moment from dusk to night. A technique for this would have been to observe the position of another celestial object to the east, while at the same time watching the sun disappear in the west. Momentarily, that object becomes a beacon of light bearing the passage of time.

Eventually that object will disappear over the horizon and another beacon of light further to the east would be chosen to take its place in the effort to continue keeping time throughout the night. At noon the next day, when the sun hangs over the southern most cavity marker, the celestial clock resets itself. The following diagram demonstrates the steps required to use the 56 burial cavities as a celestial 'compass rose', in order to determine the moment of midnight.

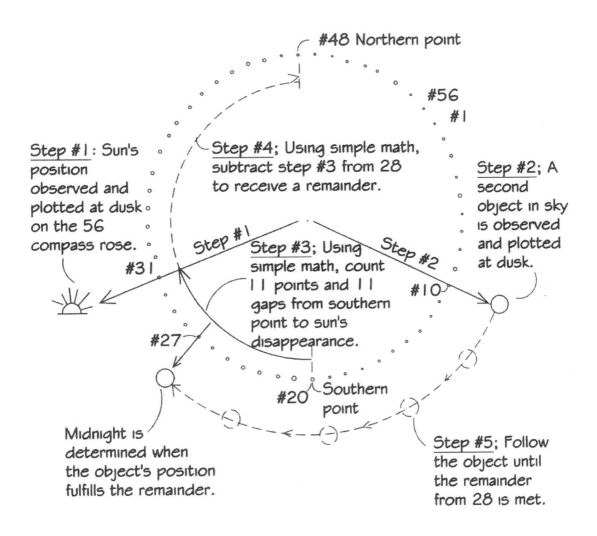

#48 Northern point

#56

#1

Step #1: Sun's position observed and plotted at dusk on the 56 compass rose.

Step #4; Using simple math, subtract step #3 from 28 to receive a remainder.

Step #2; A second object in sky is observed and plotted at dusk.

#31

Step #1

Step #3; Using simple math, count 11 points and 11 gaps from southern point to sun's disappearance.

Step #2

#10

#27

#20 Southern point

Midnight is determined when the object's position fulfills the remainder.

Step #5; Follow the object until the remainder from 28 is met.

Now that a plausible explanation into how they could determine the moment of midnight has been provided, I can fully answer the initial question of how they could determine the number of days in the orbital cycle of both Earth and Mars. Archaeologists have discovered evidence that early Pre-dynastic Egyptians determined a 365-day year by the rise and fall of the Nile River. Other cultures also performed their own experiments to determine the approximate number of days in a year. But, to determine the Martian cycle is not so easy or direct. The planet's path around the sun is elliptical and as it moves, so does the earth, along with the observer.

The following are 5 methods I believe the first inhabitants of Stonehenge could have used to determine the number of days it takes Mars to orbit around the sun, they are:

Method #1

One method would have been to count the number of oppositions of Mars while counting the number of years it takes Mars to come to opposition again in the same constellation from which the counting began. For example, if Mars starts at opposition in Sagittarius, all they would have had to do is to count the number of times Earth and Mars oppose one another until they both oppose each other again in Sagittarius. This may sound difficult, but it's not. Mars is a very erratic planet to watch, but it does have its consistencies if observed long enough. Taking a look at the diagrams provided on the following page, the reader will notice that on May 19, 3018 BCE, Mars appears at opposition (south at midnight) in the constellation of Sagittarius*. It returns to the approximate position 79 years and 3 days later.

*See reference #2.

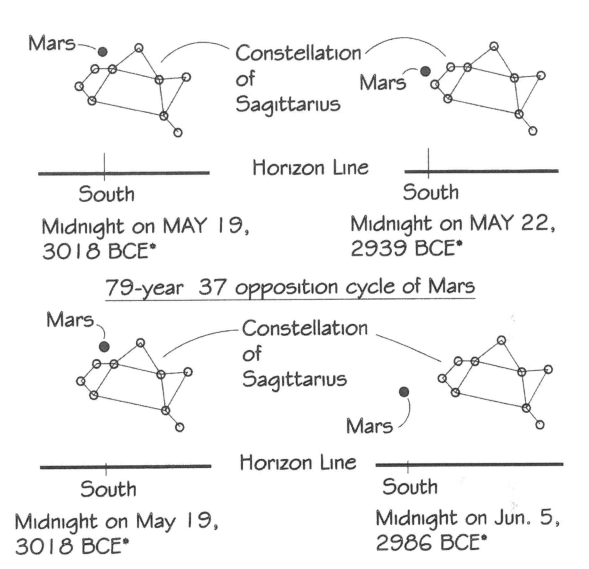

Mars— • Constellation
of
Sagittarius

Mars •

——————|—————— Horizon Line ————|————

South   South

Midnight on MAY 19,   Midnight on MAY 22,
3018 BCE*   2939 BCE*

79-year 37 opposition cycle of Mars

Mars— Constellation
of
Sagittarius

Mars • Mars

——————|—————— Horizon Line ————|————

South   South

Midnight on May 19,   Midnight on Jun. 5,
3018 BCE*   2986 BCE*

32-year 15 opposition cycle of Mars.

For this specific example, Mars was observed to appear in opposition 37 times and it took 79 years and 3 days to return to Sagittarius from which it began. Mars orbited 42 times around the Sun while Earth orbited 79 times. (79 years - 37 oppositions = 42 orbits). So, in turn, 79 years divided by 42 Martian orbits equals 1.88 years. 365 days multiplied by .88 years equals 321.2 days. 365 days plus 321.2 days equals 686.2 days. Mars must have had an orbital birthday party every 686.2 days.

*See reference #2.

It is also very probable that they only observed Mars over a period of 15 opposition occurrences, which would have been a span of approximately 32 years. If this was the case, then the math is adjusted, but the result is not significantly altered. Mars orbited 17 times around the sun while Earth orbited approximately 32 times. (32 years - 15 oppositions = 17 orbits). So, in turn, 32 years divided by 17 Martian orbits equals 1.88 years. 365 days multiplied by .88 years equals 321.2 days. 365 days plus 321.2 days equals 686.2 days. Again, Mars must have an orbital birthday every 686.2 days.

The flip-side of the math also provides the early inhabitants with the average number of days Mars would have taken to move into opposition. If in 79 years, 37 oppositions were observed, then each opposition would have taken an average of 2.135 years to occur. 365 days multiplied by 2.135 years equals 779.275 days per opposition. The result is the same for 32 years when 15 oppositions were observed.

Kepler, with all of his involved formulas, experiments, and observations determined that a Martian orbital birthday is 686.9 days. The difference of a .7-day would not have been bad for our ancestors.

Method #2

A second method would have been to utilize their observation, a coordinate system, and the average number of days in an opposition cycle. If they determined the average number of days Mars takes to opposition (about 779.2 days), their next task would have been to determine how much Mars moves from one midnight to the next. If they used a directional coordinate system of 360 degrees like that of the Sumerians, then Mars changed position each night by .462 degrees (360 degrees / 779.2 = .462 degrees). Since the constellations appear to move at a rate of .986 degrees per night, (360 degrees / 365 days = .986) they appear to pull away from Mars.

During the average number of days (779.2) it took Mars to return to opposition, the constellations appeared to have changed position approximately 768.36 degrees, (.986 x 779.2 = 768.36 degrees). During that time period, Mars only went once around the sun, so only 360 degrees of change was observed in the movement of Mars.

With the use of trial and error, they could have begun logically guessing the correct number of days in a Martian orbital cycle. Then they could have compared them to the movement in the constellations. Performing this task would have eventually provided an accurate number of days in a Martian orbital cycle. To prove this I began guessing and assumed Mars took 700 days to orbit the sun. I already knew 730 days to be false because Mars is not at opposition every two years. My examples and narratives are as follows:

Trial #1;   ⌐ (Remember, I was solving for this number).

Movement in Mars in 700 days x .462 degrees per day = 323.4 degrees;

Movement in the constellations in 700 days x .986 degree per day = 690.2 degrees. Logically, the constellations have lapped Mars by 360 degrees. I had to subtract 360 from the equation, (690.2 degrees - 360 degrees = 330.2 degrees).

Conclusion: 323.4 degrees does not equal 330.2 degrees, so I assumed the wrong number of days. The difference is 6.8 degrees.

Trial #2;

┌ (next rational guess).

Movement in Mars in 690 days x .462 degrees per day = 318.78 degrees.

Movement in constellations in 690 days x .986 degree = 680.34; - 360 = 320.34 degrees.

Conclusion: 318.78 does not equal 320.34. The difference is 1.56 degrees.

Trial #3;

┌ (next rational guess).

Movement in Mars in 688 days x .462 degrees per day = 317.85 degrees.

Movement in constellations in 688 days x .986 degree = 678.37; - 360 = 318.37 degrees.

Conclusion: 317.85 does not equal 318.37. The difference is .52 degrees.

Trial #4;

┌ (next rational guess).

Movement in Mars in 687 days x .462 degrees per day = 317.4 degrees.

Movement in constellations in 687 days x .986 degree = 677.38; - 360 = 317.38 degrees.

Conclusion: 317.394 does not exactlly equal 317.382, but it's close enough for me.

Method 3.

    A third method could have been sheer dumb luck, guesswork, and intuition. During Mars' 79-year 37 opposition cycle, there was at least one occasion when it took 779 days for Mars and Earth to reach opposition. If the inhabitants were watching during that particular cycle and made an overall assumption, then they would have been correct. But, that would have only been a 2.7 percent chance of occurring. While it would have been possible, it may not have been too probable or grounds for proof. Therefore, I will go deeper into examining the possibility of dumb luck, guesswork, and intuition.

    During this investigation another question emerged which I felt needed to be addressed. What would have been their assumed number of days in a Martian orbit for them to choose 55 or 57 spots, instead of the 56? A comparison among 55, 56, and 57 had to be evaluated to understand what may have influenced their calculations and their decision to use 56 over the other two. In other words, what Martian result is closest to Earth's 12.16-day event (365/30=12.16)? Providing this solution would strengthen the understanding into why there are 56 cavity locations equally spaced in a circular pattern, from which to bring Mars into their worship and ceremonies.

    Assuming they used the result of 12.16 for earth, it would have been to their advantage to have the estimated days in the Martian orbital cycle, divided by 55, 56, or 57 closely match 12.16. Doing so reduces the margin of error while tracking and predicting the locations of the two planets as they progress around the center of the site. Beginning with 56, the actual number of cavities found on site, and assuming 687 days in a Martian orbital cycle, I conducted the following evaluations:

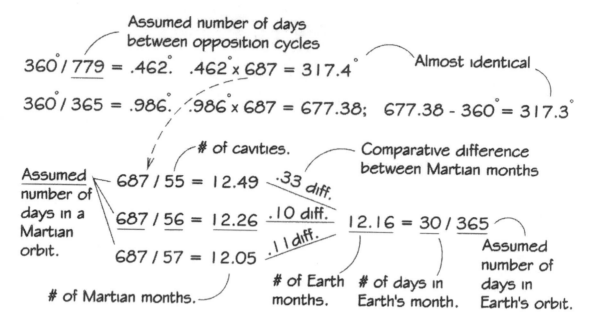

Assumed number of days
between opposition cycles

$360° / 779 = .462°$ $.462° \times 687 = 317.4°$ Almost identical

$360° / 365 = .986°$ $.986° \times 687 = 677.38;$ $677.38 - 360° = 317.3°$

\# of cavities.   Comparative difference
between Martian months

Assumed number of days in a Martian orbit.

$687 / 55 = 12.49$ $.33$ diff.

$687 / 56 = 12.26$ $.10$ diff. $12.16 = 30 / 365$

$687 / 57 = 12.05$ $.11$ diff.

\# of Martian months.   \# of Earth months.   \# of days in Earth's month.   Assumed number of days in Earth's orbit.

Conclusion: 56 is .10 (of a day) higher than 12.16, and 57 is .11 (of a day) lower than 12.16 days. So, there is only .01 (of a day) difference between choosing 56 over 57. 56 has a slight edge over 57.

Now that the equations and rational thinking have been established, I now want to examine the margin of error required to dig 55 and 57 cavities. Since there is only a .01-day difference between using 56 in lieu of 57 in the previous calculation, at what point do they flip, and using 57 becomes more advantageous?

Solving for 778 opposition days:

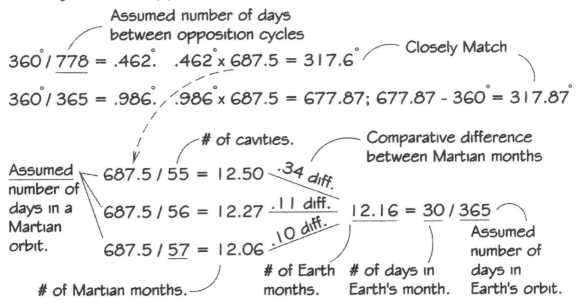

Assumed number of days between opposition cycles

$360° / \underline{778} = .462°$ $.462° \times 687.5 = 317.6°$ Closely Match

$360° / 365 = .986°$ $.986° \times 687.5 = 677.87$; $677.87 - 360° = 317.87°$

# of cavities.   Comparative difference between Martian months

Assumed number of days in a Martian orbit.

$687.5 / 55 = 12.50$ $.34$ diff.

$687.5 / 56 = 12.27$ $.11$ diff. $12.16 = \underline{30} / 365$

$687.5 / \underline{57} = 12.06$ $.10$ diff.

Assumed number of days in Earth's orbit.

# of Martian months.   # of Earth months.   # of days in Earth's month.

Conclusion: 56 is now .11 (of a day) higher than 12.16 and 57 is .10 (of a day) lower than 12.16. So, there is only .01-day difference between choosing 57 over 56. 57 now has a slight edge over 56.

I discovered it is more advantageous to dig 57 cavities, in lieu of 56, if 778 days between oppositions was assumed. Now, I have to determine the assumed number of days it would be more advantageous to dig 55 cavities.

Solving for 795 opposition days:

Assumed number of days
between opposition cycles

$360° / \underline{795} = .452°$. $.452° \times 675 = 305.66°$ Closely Match

$360° / 365 = .986°$. $.986° \times 675 = 665.55$; $665.55 - 360° = 305.55°$

# of cavities.   Comparative difference
between Martian months

Assumed number of days in a Martian orbit.

$\underline{675} / \underline{55} = 12.27$ .11 diff.

$675 / 56 = 12.05$ .11 diff. $12.16 = \underline{30} / 365$

$675 / 57 = 11.84$ .32 diff.   Assumed number of days in Earth's orbit.

# of Martian months.   # of Earth months.   # of days in Earth's month.

Conclusion: 56 is now .11 (of a day) lower than 12.16 and 55 is .11 (of a day) higher than 12.16. So, there is no difference between choosing 55 in lieu of 56. 56 has no edge over 55.

Overall Conclusion:

An observer could determine the estimated number of days in a Martian orbit by sheer dumb luck if they happen to observe a cycle that had 778 to 795 days in it. The range of the orbital cycle could have been as many as 687 and as few as 675 days, and still result in having dug 56 cavities.

The next exercise was to count the number of opposition cycles that lasted between 778 and 795 days. Using May 19, 3018 BCE, to May 19, 2939 BCE, the number of days and the dates on which they occurred are as follows:

1). March 3, 3005 BCE, to April 23, 3003 BCE;   781 days;

2). Feburary 13, 2990 BCE, to April 2, 2988 BCE;   779 days;

3). April 2, 2988 BCE, to June 6, 2986 BCE;   795 days;

4). August 24, 2984 BCE, to Oct. 11, 2982 BCE;   778 days;

5). March 8, 2973 BCE, to May 8, 2971 BCE;   791 days;

6). July 24, 2969 BCE, to Sept. 26, 2967 BCE;   794 days;

7). Feburary 20, 2958 BCE, to April 12, 2956 BCE; 781 days;

8). March 22, 2941 BCE, to May 20, 2939 BCE;   789 days;

9). Feburary 3, 2943 BCE, to March 22, 2941 BCE; 778 days.

By random observation, 9 out of 37 occurrences grants an observer a 25 percent chance of choosing an opposition event that is in the ballpark of 779.2 days. The probability is reinforced by the fact that two opposition cycles are consecutive, #2 and #3, and one of those is actually 779 days long (#2). An observer's answer could vary 12 days and still logically have dug 56 burial cavities using nothing more than a little math and a little dumb luck, guesswork, and intuition.

In addition, I also felt another question had to be answered, "Was there an advantage to having a 29 or 31-day month? First of all, being as close to a whole day is important for reducing error in time. A .16th of a day is about 3 hours and 50 minutes in a 30-day month cycle. (24 hours x 60 minutes = 1440 minutes; x .16 = 230.4 minutes; 230.4 / 60 minutes = 3 hours & 50 minutes). Whereas, 365 divided by 29 is 12.58. A .58th of a day equates to 13 hours and 55 minutes. Using 29 would have resulted in greater error in time. 31 days does not work well either. A 30-day month would have been a rational assumption on the part of the early inhabitants of Stonehenge.

Method 4.

The fourth method is by means of comparing the position of Mars against the observed changes in position of the constellations over many observations. The constellations over time appear to pull away from Mars, but both eventually disappear over the western horizon as observed at midnight. Earth and Mars are on their individual treks around the sun and the observer can use the constellations as points of reference from one observation to the next. The planets and stars appear to move quickly and slowly from east to west in our night sky. Quickly, due to the 24 hour / 360 degree counterclockwise rotation of the earth, slowly due to Earth and Mars both trekking counterclockwise around the sun. We can perceive this clearly from the 'snapshots' taken each midnight. The following is an observational case study to prove this point:

For example, in 3018 BCE Mars was seen at opposition in Sagittarius. One year later earth returned to Sagittarius but Mars was not to be found, not even on the eastern horizon. But, more often then not, it would show up in Gemini on the western horizon, just after sunset. Gemini is opposite Sagittarius on the constellation rose.

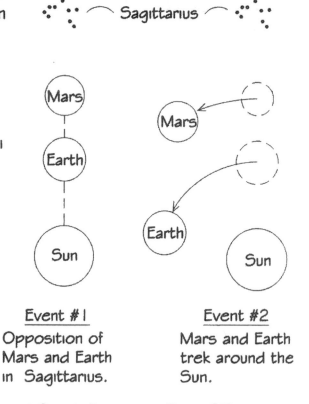

Event #1
Opposition of
Mars and Earth
in Sagittarius.

Event #2
Mars and Earth
trek around the
Sun.

Two years (730 days) after the previous opposition, Sagittarius became south once again, meaning that earth completed a second full orbit around the sun. Mars however, could usually be seen on the eastern horizon in a constellation two over from the left of the previous opposition constellation. In this case, two over from the left of Sagittarius is the constellation of Aquarius. Logically at some point, Mars must have met up and then passed the constellation of Sagittarius along its trek around the sun. Mars would have completed one lap around the sun plus two additional constellations into its next orbital lap. Eventually, Earth and Mars met up again for their next opposition in the constellation of Pisces, one to the left of Aquarius. The following diagrams support this description:

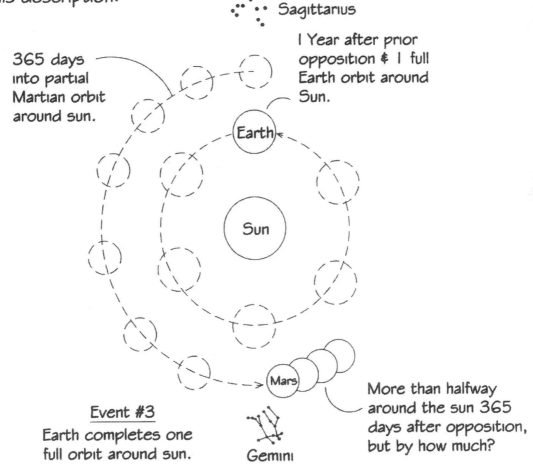

Earth & Mars on day 365

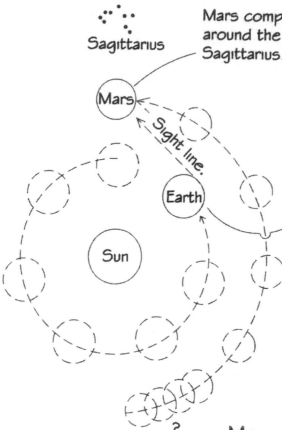

Mars completes one full orbit around the sun when it returns to Sagittarius. How many days is this?

Earth is due to complete a second trek around the Sun on the day Mars completes its first. Sometimes Mars can be seen in the previous opposition constellation on the eastern horizon at midnight.

Event #4

Mars moves into Sagittarius completing one full orbit around sun.

Mars completes one orbit

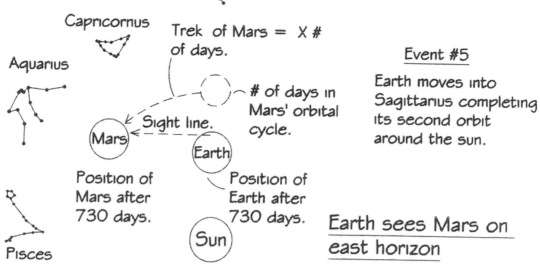

Sagittarius

Capricornus

Aquarius

Trek of Mars = X # of days.

# of days in Mars' orbital cycle.

Sight line.

Position of Mars after 730 days.

Position of Earth after 730 days.

Pisces

Event #5

Earth moves into Sagittarius completing its second orbit around the sun.

Earth sees Mars on east horizon

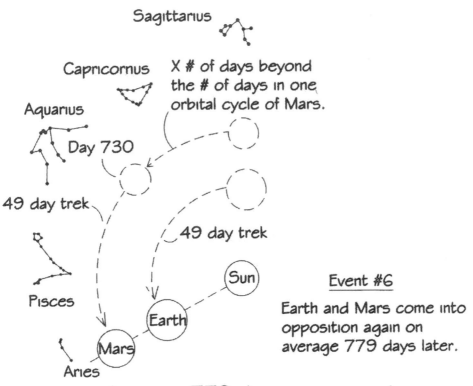

Sagittarius

Capricornus

X # of days beyond the # of days in one orbital cycle of Mars.

Aquarius

Day 730

49 day trek

49 day trek

Pisces

Sun

Earth

Event #6

Earth and Mars come into opposition again on average 779 days later.

Mars

Aries

Average 779 days per opposition

So, what can be determined from this simplistic description in order to develop a logical solution? I know that one is equal to two, three, and maybe even four. It means Mars does not appear south at midnight when Earth completes its 365, 730, or 1,095-day orbit. If we could see Mars through daylight while Earth returns to Sagittarius one year later, it would appear to us along with the morning sun. It then would trek through the day along with the sun. Usually it is behind the sun and can be seen on the horizon after sunset, but sometimes it reaches the horizon ahead of the sun. Being able to see Mars after sunset assures the observer that it has gone more than halfway around the sun 365 days later.

If Mars were exactly halfway around the sun in its orbit when earth returned to Sagittarius, then Mars would always return to it every two years. But it does not. Mars' orbit is erratic, but it always passes the previous opposition constellation before earth completes its second trip. Mars must be more than halfway counterclockwise around the sun after a 365-day orbit. But by how much?

The solution to that question can be determined by observations made between the time Mars was sighted in Sagittarius to the time Mars and Earth reach their following opposition in Aries.

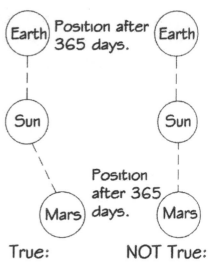

On day 365

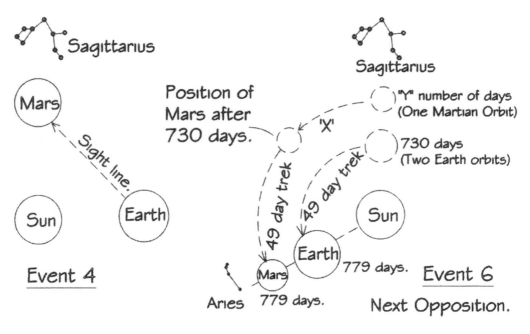

Event 4

Event 6

Next Opposition.

Attempting to solve the question by simply counting the number of days between the time Mars is seen in Sagittarius to the time earth reaches Sagittarius will not work. The sight lines are at an angle and both planets are traveling in arced elliptical orbits. But once earth reaches Sagittarius on day 730, the observer can begin counting the number of days until the next opposition.

On average, Earth and Mars align at opposition 779 days after the previous opposition. With this information the observer can assume both planets traveled for 49 days, and Mars traveled an additional 49 days after Earth was in Sagittarius. The math for Earth is straightforward: 779 days - 49 days = 730 days. To solve for Mars, the observer has to think in terms of the past: 779 days - 49 days - 'X' days, brings Mars back to the same point as Earth on day 730.

If the observer does not assume that Mars changed its course or speed between the time of its orbital birthday to the time it met up with Earth again at opposition, the parameters of 'X' number of days are the same as the parameters of the 49 days. If so, then 779 days - 49 days - 49 days equals a Martian orbit of 681 days.

But, there is a problem; the Martian orbital cycle is not twice as fast as Earth's, so the answer of 681 days is incorrect. The time it takes Mars to reach Sagittarius is fewer than two orbits of Earth and greater than fifty percent of Mars' orbit is equal to one orbit of Earth. If one is equal to 730 days then Mars' orbital cycle has to be fewer than one, so in turn, 50% (.5) of Mars' orbit must be fewer than 365 days. To get my head around the math, I had to make the following chart for Mars' orbit:

If .49 is = to 357.7 days, then 1.0 is = to 715.4; Loss of 14.6 days.
If .48 is = to 350.4 days, then 1.0 is = to 700.8; Loss of 29.4 days.
If .47 is = to 343.1 days, then 1.0 is = to 686.2; Loss of 43.8 days.
If .46 is = to 335.8 days, then 1.0 is = to 671.6; Loss of 58 days.

I provided myself a rational and logical limited range of days in which to determine the correct answer. In order to narrow it, additional assumptions had to be made. The observer has never seen Mars equal to or fewer than one constellation to the left of the previous opposition constellation upon Earth's second passing, if each constellation is about 30 days long, (365 / 12 = 30.4) then .49 and .48 must be removed from the chart.

If .47 is = to 343.1 days, then 1.0 is = to 686.2; Loss of 43.8 days.
If .46 is = to 335.8 days, then 1.0 is = to 671.6; Loss of 58 days.

It has been determined that 681 days is incorrect. Are there too many days or too few? The assumption that Mars travels 98 days (49 +49) from Sagittarius has to be incorrect. If one is fewer than 730 and .5 fewer than 365, then 98 has be fewer than 98, thus making the correct answer greater than 681 days (779 - 97 is greater than 681). Per the chart, if the answer is greater than 681 then .46 must be removed from the chart also. Only .47 on the chart remains, thus the assumed number of days in Mars' orbit is 686.2 days.

If .47 is = to 343.1 days, then 1.0 is = to 686.2; Loss of 43.8 days.

Method 5

I believe they also could have used ground markers to track and gauge the change in position of the stars and planets. Julian Richards, author of English Heritage Guidebook, discusses a timber phase constructed after the digging and shaping of the circular mounds.⟨10⟩ Also, Christopher Chippindale in his book, Stonehenge Complete, includes a plan of holes titled, "Phase 2",⟨11⟩ which closely matches that of Julian Richards' sketch showing standing posts and fencing material.

I believe the builders used techniques to investigate their world while occupying this site and during the time period of its construction. If not, then they brought the information with them and the connection between the 56 cavities and Mars just simply appeared on the site. If that were the case, then it would reinforce the argument that the builders where studying their surroundings long before construction began at Stonehenge.

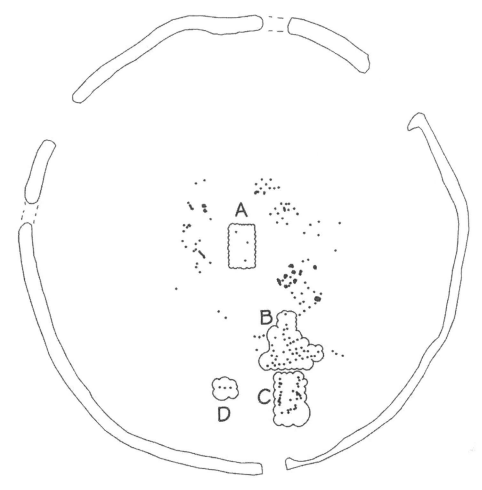

<u>Variety of holes located on the site</u>

I do not support the theory that the holes were used for fencing, I believe their purpose was to track the movements of celestial bodies in the night sky.

As an architect, I saw the holes in associated groups, such as the three at the center of the site, I called those, 'Group A' on the diagram. Three other clusters of holes interested me. I identified each of them with a letter calling them, 'B', 'C', and 'D'. I believe group 'A' could have been used as centering points for the other three groups.

Examining hole locations in Group 'B' more closely, I noticed that some points are just slightly off from the next, all in a row. Architecturally, this produces a wall of 'offset' points when viewed from a centering point located in Group 'A'. A system like that can be used to home-in on a specific star or planet. Holes spread further apart can mark the passing of weeks or days, while tightly aligned holes can mark the passing of hours or minutes. Looking at Group 'B', I labeled the eastern most hole on the diagram as 'hold point B1'. From that point an observer could have determined 12 degrees of change in a star's position over 30 consecutive nights. 30 days x 12 degrees = 360 degrees and 30 tallies of 12.16 days = 365 days.

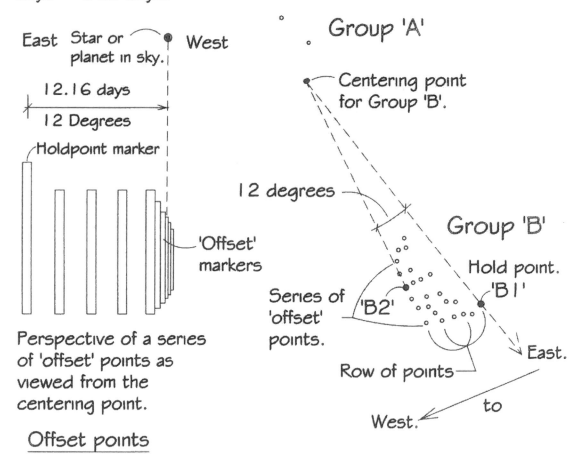

East   Star or   West
       planet in sky.

12.16 days

12 Degrees

Holdpoint marker

'Offset' markers

Perspective of a series of 'offset' points as viewed from the centering point.

Offset points

Group 'A'

Centering point for Group 'B'.

12 degrees

Group 'B'

Hold point. 'B1'

Series of 'offset' points.

'B2'

East.

Row of points

West.   to

Once Earth's 12-degree 30-day increment was established, they could find out how many degrees Mars moved during that time period. I believe Group 'C' served that purpose since the point I perceived as the hold point for the group, is almost directly in line with marker 'B2'. In addition, the difference between 'C1' and 'C2' is 6.42 degrees, which is almost 1/56th of a circle.

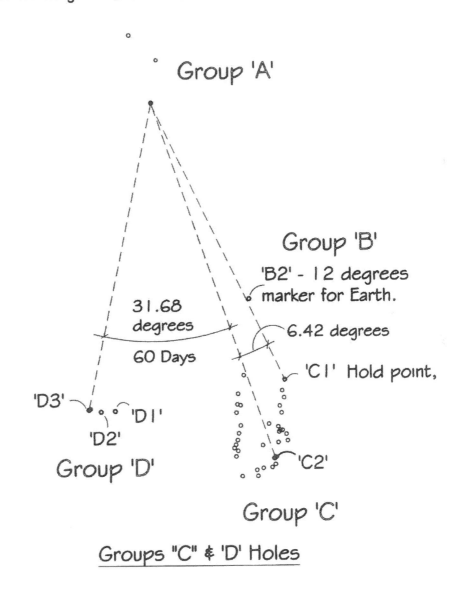

Groups "C" & 'D' Holes

I have provided 5 plausible methods in which the early inhabitants of Stonehenge could have determined a ballpark estimate of the number of days in Mars' orbital year around the sun. Providing these methods supports my theory that it is very plausible the 56 burial cavities were used to mark the passing of time, particularly in 12.16-day increments in order to track the progress of Mars. Their invention provided themselves an invaluable time keeping mechanism, along with a greater understanding of the world around them.

I also imagine Mars as a religious event, connecting souls to the greater universe. Upon the death of an important member of their society, I believe their cremated remains would have been placed in a burial cavity associated with the timing of their death with respect to Mars' position along its trek around the sun; forever solidifying them among the stars. Egyptians used this cosmology widely in their death rituals.

But, additional questions would eventually have to be answered by the observer, such as, "Why is Mars so erratic in its timing around the sun"? "Is it Mars or is the problem with Earth's orbit"? They already dug the cavities for Mars, so the orbital correction may have to be solved when they create Earth's orbital pits, right? I believe I have found evidence that the early eras of Stonehenge used the planetary chart to attempt to answer these questions. I will provide that information later in the book.

Grand Sarsens: Chapter 4

For many, this site is about the raising and stacking of extremely large stones for unknown or mystical purposes. As a previous visitor to the site, I felt a little reluctant to reveal my findings for fear of tarnishing the alluring qualities of the ancient structure. But, as an architect, I've been impatient to explain the purpose of the taller stones (sarsens) erected at the center and those which form the outer ring. I have interpreted the term sarsen to mean a large boulder of rock found laying above the ground in England.

With fresh perspective and no preconceived assumptions, I asked the stones the following questions, "Why are the upright standing stones capped with a horizontal lintel? "What was the significance of such unique construction and why was this site so special? "What was the significance of the uniquely chiseled and specially crafted sloping sides of the sarsens, and why do the gaps between two standing stones form a 'V' shaped triangle?" "What was so important in their design intent to validate the added labor in locating, transporting, lifting, setting, and shaping 35 additional stones?

During my research, I could not find another historical example of this type of construction, particularly one that provides for a lintel with a longer span than was absolutely necessary to carry a load to the foundation. The builders of Stonehenge chipped away at the stones after they were set into place making the lintels longer than they had to be. This type of construction is counterintuitive to safety and structural design. Assuming the lintels were not provided merely for decoration, there had to have been a profound and justifiable purpose for this type of construction.

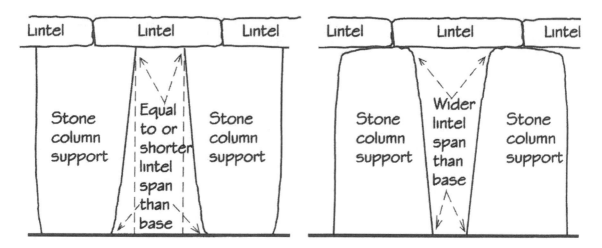

Intuitive transfer of structural load to foundation

Counterintuitive transfer of structural load to foundation

While visiting the interior of the site for the first time in the summer of 2015 CE it was surprising to experience how cluttered, confined, and obstructed the center of the site is. It is evident to me that the site was not designed to be viewed exclusively from the center. It was a structure in which the astronomer must move around and walk among the stones in order to see the celestial alignments.

The answers to the previous questions became apparent once explored. The stones framed a permanent view, but a view to what? Since the gaps between the stones form a 'V', it is evident that the view at the top is more important than the view at the bottom. With the addition of a capping lintel, the view became framed in on all four sides. The astronomer could include or exclude elements in the night sky at their choosing.

It is not so evident now that the ground has several inches of dirt supporting grass and the stones are weathered and dull, but in the beginning, the entire area would have reflected light from the layer of white chalk presently underneath the soil. The structure and ground would have been much more reflective. The early users of the structure could have easily performed their observations during the darkest of nights. It is clear that this structure was designed and intended to be used primarily to view the night sky and to a lesser degree, for watching solar events.

Further peeling the historical onion of Stonehenge, I begin by discussing the 10 standing sarsens configured in a 'U' shaped pattern surrounding the center of the structure. Based on my investigation and explanation to their purpose and significance, I believe they were constructed before the 30 shorter standing sarsens which make up the outer ring of stones. Using poetic license once again, I assumed their completion date on May 5, 2687 BCE, while Mars was at opposition in Sagittarius*. This date is also in the ballpark of the generally accepted date of construction provided by many archaeologists. The star alignments I discovered also confirm the dating of structure, thus supporting the results of their carbon dating techniques.

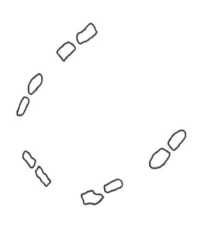

5 sets of inner sarsens

On closer examination, the plan configuration takes on an uncanny resemblance to that of the star patterns found in the constellation of Sagittarius. I chose to begin the 79-year 37 opposition cycles of Mars on May 19, 3018 BCE, because Mars was positioned at opposition directly outside the second star in the 'tea pot' of Sagittarius.

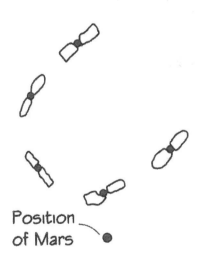

Position of Mars

Portals as star pattern

Once I recognized the simularites between star patterns in Sagittarius with that of the stones, I overlaid the two in plan. Sagittarius has two 'U' shaped configurations, the 'Tea Pot' and 'Lagoon Nebula'. After rotating and mirroring both patterns, I concluded that the builders used a generic stone pattern which would capture their intended views between the stones while symbolizing Sagittarius. Astronomers have discovered that the Lagoon Nebula is the center of the Milky Way and our galaxy. ⟨9⟩ Doing so would have represented Stonehenge as the 'center' here on earth.

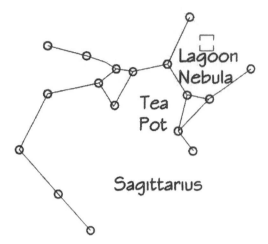

Sagittarius

Tea Pot VS.
Lagoon Nebula:

Over-lay: Tea Pot

Over-lay: Lagoon Nebula

Sagittarius at
the navel of the
Goddess Nut.

Standing Nut 12

The Maya also knew of the importance of Sagittarius and I found it interesting that Nut, the Egyptian goddess of the Mily Way and night sky, had Sagittarius at her navel.

While attempting to answer how the stone structure could have been used to gauge the direction of south, I found that stone #11 is the southern most standing stone in the ring of sarsens. It was also shaped much differently than the others. It is much shorter, thinner, and it has a rounded top. I felt this was important some how. Then it hit me like my mother's flyswatter. While drawing on the plan, I noticed that a line taken from the center of the site ran between stone #53 and #54 and directly across stone #11. After my site visit, I can now state that these three stones were used as a 'V' shaped portal for which to view planetary opposition. Stone #11 was used as a gnomon for which to locate the direction of south.

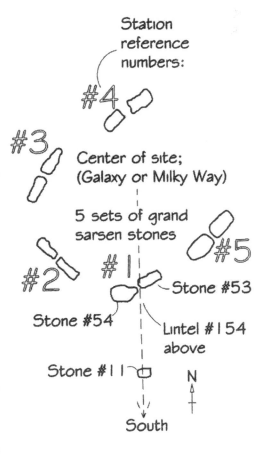

Station reference numbers:

#4

#3

Center of site; (Galaxy or Milky Way)

5 sets of grand sarsen stones

#2

#1

#5

Stone #53

Stone #54

Lintel #154 above

Stone #11

N

South

Grand sarsen plan

It was interesting to notice that station #1 on my plan, stones #53, #54, and #154 appear very different compared to the other four sets of grand sarsens. After 4,700 years they still look grand, monumental, and brand-new. The edges on the lintel have remained crisp and sharp while those on the other grand sarsens look very weathered and eroded.

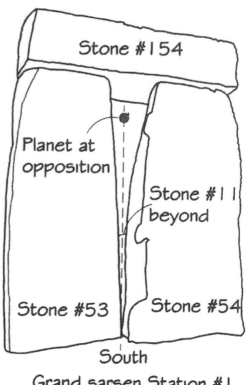

Grand sarsen Station #1

In order to solidify that this was their new tool to gauge planetary opposition, a few more questions had to be answered. Was the structure's gap tall enough to see the planets while they were at their highest and lowest points in the sky? Would the lintel on the outer ring of sarsens block the view of low passing planets?

The section below demonstrates that it is not possible to see 25 degrees above the horizon from the center of the site. During my research I learned that the planets range between 13 and 67 degrees above the horizon. In order to see planets above the outer lintel, the astronomer would have had to move toward the grand sarenes.

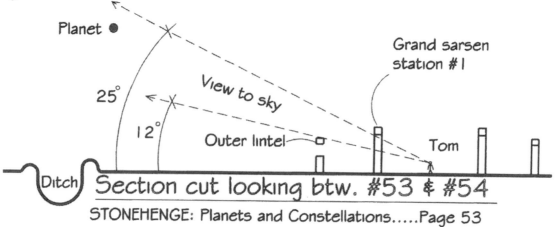

Section cut looking btw. #53 & #54

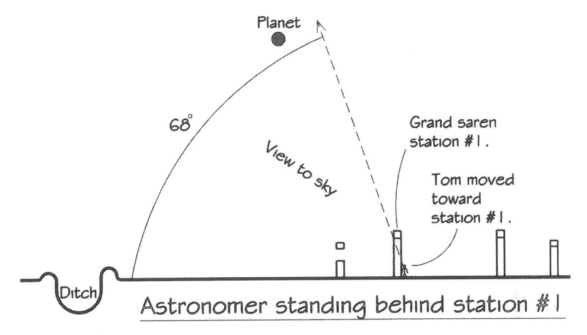

Planet

68°

View to sky

Grand saren
station #1.

Tom moved
toward
station #1.

Ditch

Astronomer standing behind station #1

The section above demonstrates that an ancient astronomer would have been able to see the planets at their highest position in the sky and remain behind the structure.

Now that there was a purpose for the sarsens at station #1, what was the purpose of the other four? To help answer this question, I began comparing the heights of their lintels. The lintel of station #4 and #5 are both about 20 feet, the lintel of station #1 and #3 are both about 22 feet, and the lintel of station #2 would have been about 24 feet above the ground. It was as if the top of one lintel was the same height as the bottom of the next lintel as they stair-stepped toward the apex. I thought to myself, "If one set of sarsens was dedicated for watching planets, then the other four may have been dedicated to watching the stars, but which stars"?

The answer to my question came by pure luck and observation. While studying Mars and planetary opposition, I noticed that Deneb, a star in the constellation of Cygnus appeared south on July 17, 2687 BCE.* It was fantastic to finally have a star appear between the stones at midnight, but at the time, I did not realize July 17th was the summer solstice for that era. Our summer solstice presently occurs on June 21st, but because of axial procession, the date changes over time.

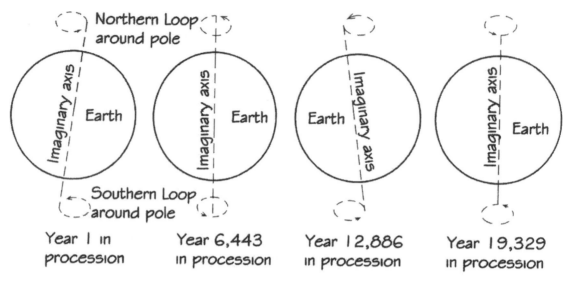

Year 1 in procession

Year 6,443 in procession

Year 12,886 in procession

Year 19,329 in procession

Axial procession

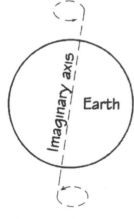

Year 25,772 in procession

As I understand it, procession is a term that describes the axis of earth looping around the north and south pole. The poles are not pinned to one specific point in space. Over approximately 25,770 years, they loop in a gigantic circle and return back to an original starting point. It is because of procession that our perspective of the positions of the stars change over time.

*See Reference note #2;
    STONEHENGE: Planets and Constellations.....Page 55

Axial procession is the reason the star we now call the North Star has not always been the North Star. Over long periods of time the star that receives the title changes. Polaris, located in the Little Dipper is the North Star today, but in 2687 BCE the North Star was Thuban, which is located in the constellation of Draco.*

Examining the grand sarsen plan more closely, I began studying its geometry for clues to possible alignments. I determined that an early astronomer could see through all five gaps while standing at the center of the site. After calculating their angles I compared them to the dates when Deneb could have been seen through each of the gaps at midnight throughout 2687 BCE.

I believe Deneb and the constellation of Cygnus would have been chosen to watch because, at that time, Cygnus was visible at midnight all year-round while all other constellations disappeared below the horizon. In addition, Deneb was easy to see since it did not get too high above the horizon throughout the year. These qualities would have made a good star and constellation to gauge time with. To understand this concept and their celestial invention is to understand Stonehenge at midnight.

335° 0° North alignment
Dec. 16th
#4 — Station reference.
275° #3
Sept. 17th
#5
230° #2 #1 121°
August 6th June 21st
178°
July 17th
N

Alignments with
Deneb 2687 BCE

*See Reference note #2;

Puzzled at what I had found, I began researching documents from ancient cultures and came across a festival calendar used in ancient Egypt. After comparing my research to the calendar, I noticed that dates of alignments correlated with important festivals. For example, during the week of the summer solstice, July 13th to the 18th, marked the last few days of the year. Egyptians called this week the, "Epagomenal Days".** Each day signified the birthday of an important god in their religion, July 13th was the birthday of Ra;** July 14th was the birthday of Osiris (Wasir);** July 15 was the birthday of Heru-Dunawhy;** July 16 was the Birthday of Set;** July 17 was the birthday of Isis;** and July 18 was the birthday of Nephthys.** But, July 19 was the first day of the first month of their new year, which they called Thoth.**

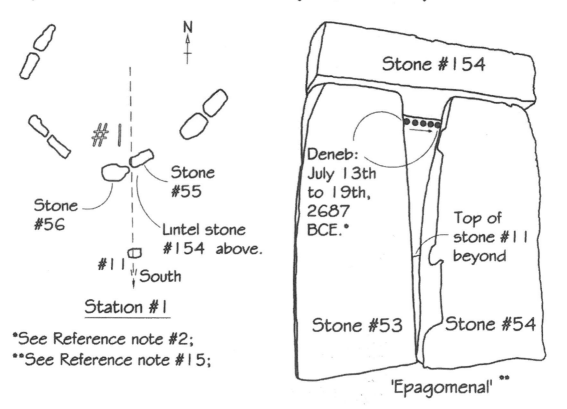

N

#1

Stone
#55

Stone
#56

Lintel stone
#154 above.

#11

South

Station #1

*See Reference note #2;
**See Reference note #15;

Stone #154

Deneb:
July 13th
to 19th,
2687
BCE.*

Top of
stone #11
beyond

Stone #53

Stone #54

'Epagomenal' **

The upper portion of the gap is very wide, which told me that they were able to see Deneb under the lintel for an entire week at midnight, marking the celebration of the birthdays of the gods.

STONEHENGE: Planets and Constellations.....Page 57

Remembering that Stonehenge has deposits of cremated remains, it was uncanny to find Deneb appear between the stones on August 4th and 6th. Those dates were associated with the Festival of the Dead and to Nut,** the goddess of the Milky Way.

Continuing clockwise to station #3, an ancient astronomer could have seen Deneb at 275 degrees on September 17th* between stones #57 and #58, marking the first day in the Egyptian month of Hathor.** Since this angle is not perpendicular to the back of the stones and the five stations are elongated along a central axis, I chose to draw two additional circles bisecting all their openings. Deneb was now able to be seen at 295 degrees on October 17th* from point 'B', which began the month of Koiak.**

Stone #58

#2

Stone #57

Lintel #156 above.

Station #2

*See note #2.

**See note #15.

Nov. 6th -10th @ 307° - 310°**

C

Oct. 17th @ 295°**
Start of Koiak** B

Sept. 17th @ 275°**
Start of Hethara** A

#3

#58

#57

O° North alignment
O

Central Axis

Added circles.

A

C

B

N

Station #3

From point 'C', Deneb would have been seen at 307, 308, and 310 degrees on the dates of November 6th, 7th, and 10th* signaling the respective Egyptian festivals of 'Raising the Djed Pillar',** 'Ploughing the Earth',** and 'Sokar'.**

STONEHENGE: Planets and Constellations.....Page 58

The ability to view Deneb at midnight was coming to a close at Stonehenge. Cygnus, 'The Swan' was descending and would eventually disappear beneath the horizon for several months. But not before it was seen from several vantage points between stones #59 and #60. While standing at point 'D', the observer would have seen Deneb on November 16th at 314 degrees,* which began the month of Tybi.** Then, from the center of the site at point 'E', it would have been seen on December 16th at 335 degrees,* which began Mechir.** Finally, on December 25th it would have looked as if the swan landed and come to nest in the northern barrow in celebration for the birthday of Horus.**

At this time of year, Deneb would have been so low on the horizon that lintel #160 would not have been needed. Why was it constructed?

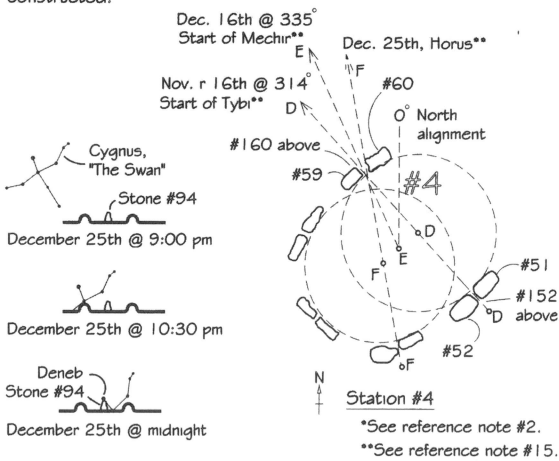

Dec. 16th @ 335°
Start of Mechir**
E

Dec. 25th, Horus**
F

Nov. r 16th @ 314°
Start of Tybi**
D

#60

0° North
alignment

#160 above

Cygnus,
"The Swan"

Stone #94

December 25th @ 9:00 pm

#59

#4

D

E

F

#51

#152
D above

#52

F

December 25th @ 10:30 pm

Deneb
Stone #94

December 25th @ midnight

N

Station #4

*See reference note #2.

**See reference note #15.

STONEHENGE: Planets and Constellations.....Page 59

My imagination goes as far as to plot the Milky Way across the site with Sagittarius and the Lagoon Nebula placed at the center, thus making Stonehenge the center of the Milky Way here on earth.

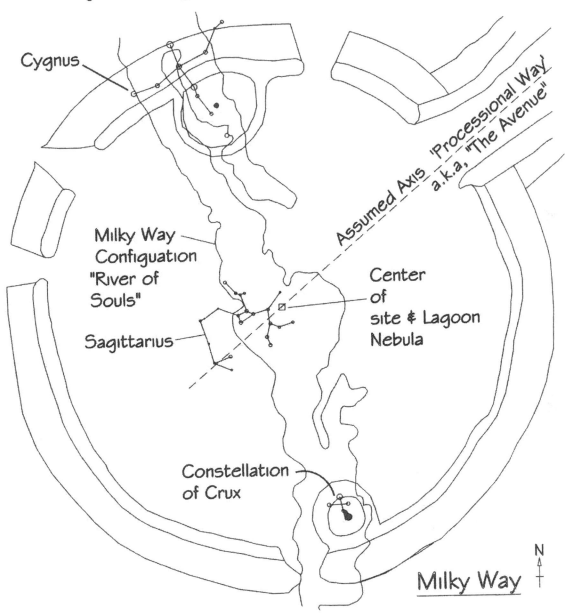

Cygnus

Milky Way Configuation "River of Souls"

Sagittarius

Assumed Axis 'Processional Way' a.k.a, "The Avenue"

Center of site & Lagoon Nebula

Constellation of Crux

N

Milky Way

It just so happens that Cygnus and Crux each land in a barrow. I believed they used the seasonal position of the Milky Way to help gauge the timing of the seasons and incorporated it into their religious events.

STONEHENGE: Planets and Constellations.....Page 60

If the northern barrow was built to nest Cygnus, then was the southern barrow designed for Crux? The answer came several years after asking the question. Stonehenge taught me an understanding between the Milky Way and the 12 Zodiac constellations. I developed the following diagrams which I hope will help you.

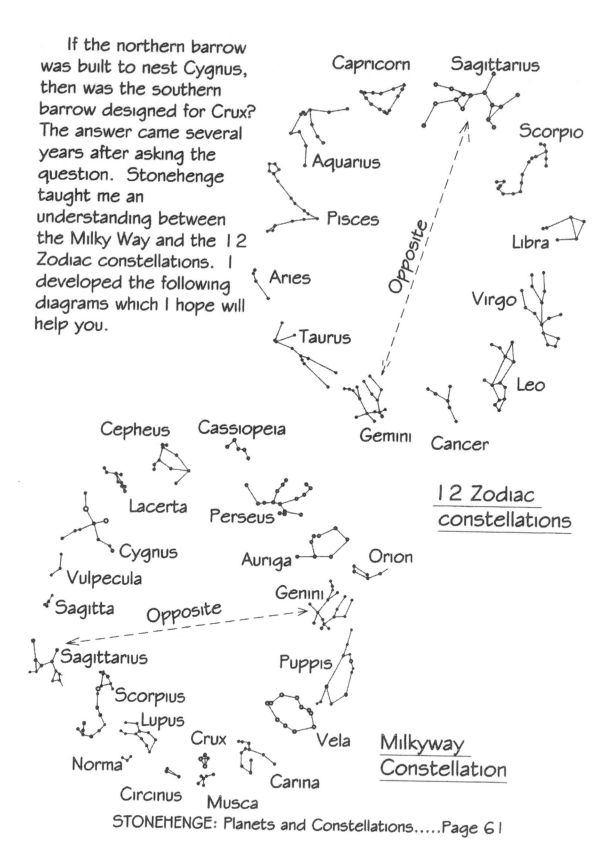

Capricorn

Sagittarius

Aquarius

Scorpio

Pisces

Libra

Aries

Virgo

Opposite

Taurus

Leo

Gemini   Cancer

12 Zodiac constellations

Cepheus   Cassiopeia

Lacerta   Perseus

Cygnus   Auriga   Orion

Vulpecula

Sagitta   Opposite   Genini

Sagittarius   Puppis

Scorpius

Lupus

Crux   Vela

Norma

Milkyway Constellation

Circinus   Musca   Carina

STONEHENGE: Planets and Constellations.....Page 61

I learned, schematically speaking, that there are two loops of constellations that ring our view in the night sky. One contain the constellations located within the Milky Way and the other are those that fall along the path of the sun called the zodiac. Clarity came with studying each and finding that Sagittarius and Gemini are opposite each other on both of the diagrams. Tilting the diagram in different directions will help you better understand the tilting and orbiting of the earth in relation to the nightly view.

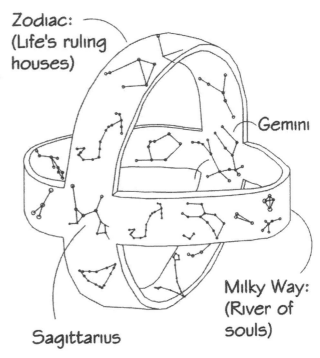

Zodiac: (Life's ruling houses)

Gemini

Sagittarius

Milky Way: (River of souls)

The symbol of earth is usually shown as two crossed lines dividing a circle into four quadrants. Some authors state that it represents our longitude and latitude coordinates. Gavin White suggests that it represents the, "year divided by the solstices and equinoxes".⟨77⟩ I believe it was developed as a diagrammatic concept of the meeting place of the two constellations.

Earth

Having new understand of the Milky Way and how it can be over head during the summer and sitting on the horizon during the winter, I discovered that on February 9, 2687 BCE* Crux appeared from the southern barrow at midnight. That was the, "Day of unseen in the Underworld".**

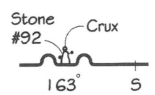

Stone #92 — Crux

163°   S

Southern barrow on Feb. 9, 2687 BCE

*See note #2; **See note #15;

During that time period, the Milky Way (River of Souls) sat and surrounded the horizon. It would have been a powerful and moving experience to behold. The connection between Crux and the southern barrow could have been a gateway from which to release souls from the underworld into the cosmos.

Deneb would have appeared from its dormancy on February 13th, in time to venerate the day that the, "Doorways of the Horizon were Open".** Marrying the date of that festival, with the imagery of the Milky Way surrounding the horizon and the series of openings in the structure, is absolutely uncanny.

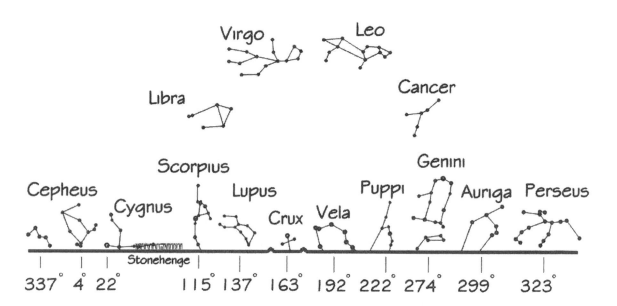

The remaining grand sarsen stones left to discuss are stones #51, #52, and lintel #152 at Station #5 on my plan. Deneb would have appeared on or about February 9th, at approximately 19 degrees.* On June 14th Deneb would have appeared between stones #51 and #52 indicating the first day of Mesore, the last month in the Egyptian calendar.** Then, a few days later, an astronomer would have moved to the center of the site to witness Deneb between the stones on June 21st. That would have marked the day of the Wadjet Ceremony. Lastly, July 2nd would have indicated the "Eye of the Wadjet" festival.**

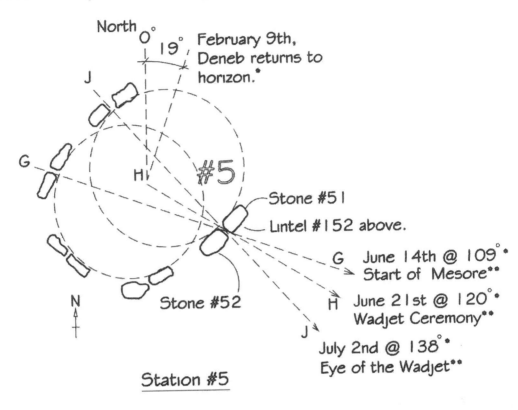

North 0°

19' February 9th,
Deneb returns to
horizon.*

J

G

H #5

Stone #51

Lintel #152 above.

N

Stone #52

G June 14th @ 109°*
→ Start of Mesore**

H June 21st @ 120°*
→ Wadjet Ceremony**

J
↘ July 2nd @ 138°*
Eye of the Wadjet**

Station #5

After studying the degree angles of smaller stones that still remain on site between sarsen #60 and #51 and four holes at the mouth of the 'Processional Way', may shed light on their original purpose as they relate to Deneb. The Egyptian month of Parmutit began on February 14th** when Deneb was at 23 degrees*. The month of Pachons began on March 16th** with Deneb at 44 degrees.* The following month of Payni began on April 15th** with Deneb at 64 degrees* and finally, the month of Epipi began on May 15** while Deneb was at 83 degrees.* There were several notable festivals in the month of Pachons,** which have hole designations at the mouth entering the 'Processional Way'.

*See reference note #2;
**See reference note #15;
STONEHENGE: Planets and Constellations.....Page 64

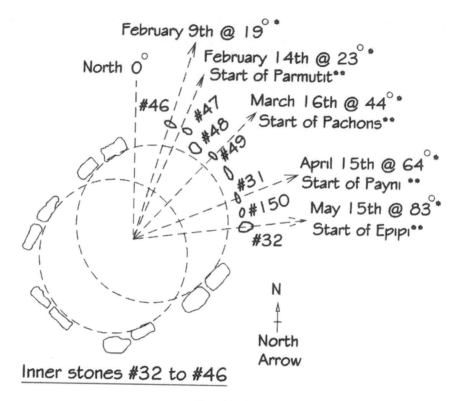

February 9th @ 19°*

February 14th @ 23°*
Start of Parmutit**

North 0°

#46

#47

#48

March 16th @ 44°*
Start of Pachons**

#49

#31

April 15th @ 64°*
Start of Payni **

#150

May 15th @ 83°*
Start of Epipi**

#32

N
↑
+
North
Arrow

Inner stones #32 to #46

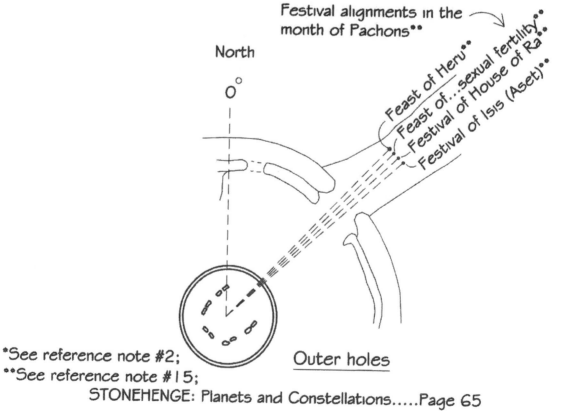

Festival alignments in the
month of Pachons**

North

0°

Feast of Heru**

Feast of...sexual fertility**

Festival of House of Ra**

Festival of Isis (Aset)**

Outer holes

*See reference note #2;
**See reference note #15;
   STONEHENGE: Planets and Constellations.....Page 65

Orbit of Halley's Comet: Chapter 5

I turn my attention to the purpose of the arc of shorter stones located among the 'U' shaped grand sarsen configuration. Their construction is also interesting. Each stone's height is about 3 inches different from one to the next as they symmetrically stair-step up to the center of the arc. Researchers have estimated that there used to be 19 stones. Only about half of the stones remain. I was baffled for a long time regarding their purpose, but now I believe they represented a memory of Halley's Comet.

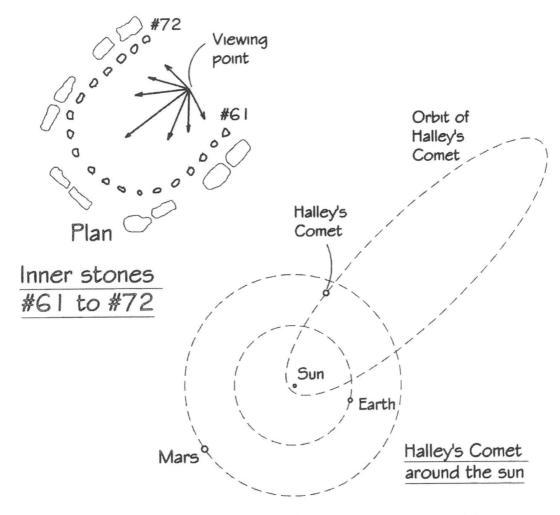

#72

Viewing point

#61

Plan

Inner stones
#61 to #72

Orbit of Halley's Comet

Halley's Comet

Sun

Earth

Mars

Halley's Comet around the sun

The reason I'm having a bit of fun with these stones comes from the time I came across photos taken of the comet between April 26 and June 11, 1910.[16] They were arranged by date, one next to the other. What impressed me was the fact that the tail in each picture was longer than the previous. As the comet approached the sun, the tail increased in length. The series of pictures also showed the tail decrease in length as the comet moved away from the sun. As a comet moves closer to the sun the tail becomes longer from dust and gas being affected by the Sun's radiation. As it travels away, the tail begins to decrease.

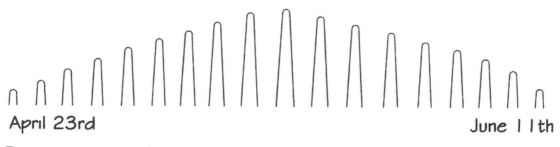

April 23rd   June 11th

Representation of a series of photos from 1910 of Halley's Comet

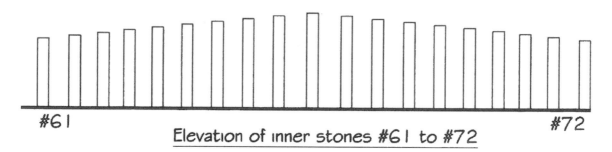

#61   #72

Elevation of inner stones #61 to #72

I recognized the same imagery in the arc of stones. The closer they got to the center, the taller they became. If the stones were observed from #61 around to #72, then it would symbolize the comet approaching and leaving the sun.

For example, during 1985 and 1986 the comet passed through our system. During that time, several movies were made describing death with the arrival of the comet. Our early ancestors

STONEHENGE: Planets and Constellations.....Page 67

may have also seen the coming of the comet associated with omens. The stone I believe proves my theory is #68. It is one of the tallest in the arc and someone took the time to carve along its length. With sun on the stone, it looks strikingly similar to several of the pictures taken in 1910.

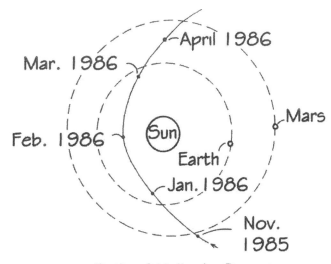

Path of Halley's Comet
1985 to 1986 CE. 7

Head of Halley's Comet

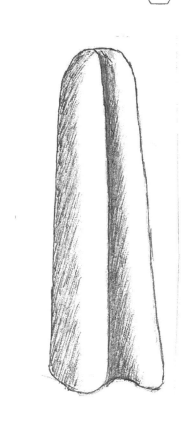

Stone #68

STONEHENGE: Planets and Constellations.....Page 68

The Sarsen Ring: Chapter 6

Even before digging the first hole to place the first sarsen, the builders had to have a plan for construction. A plan for how wide the structure was to be, the size and height of each stone, and how many it would take to complete the design. As an architect, the simplest questions can be the easiest to overlook because the answer may be grounded in assumption.

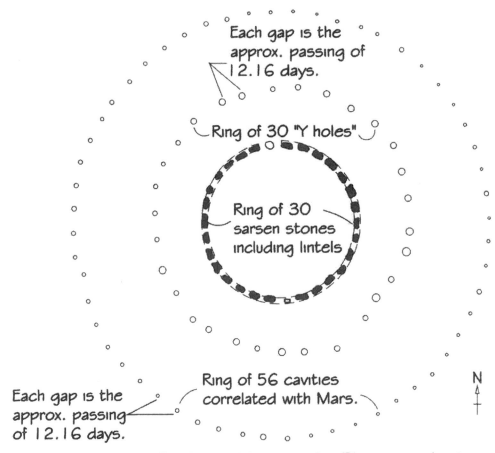

Each gap is the approx. passing of 12.16 days.

Ring of 30 "Y holes"

Ring of 30 sarsen stones including lintels

Each gap is the approx. passing of 12.16 days.

Ring of 56 cavities correlated with Mars.

N

Earth and Mars on the Planetary chart

As discussed, the width and height of the structure was based on site proportions and a step-down ratio of time. The advantage of the design enabled an ancient astrologer and astronomer to predict the timing of Mars in their night sky.

STONEHENGE: Planets and Constellations.....Page 69

As Mars and Earth trek around the sun, Mars will eventually depart from our night sky for several months because of the sun's rays and the bright blue sky of daylight. Mars is still there, but it cannot be seen. Over time, the two planets change position and Mars returns to view before the morning sun on the eastern horizon. Each day Mars will appear for a longer period of time, when eventually, it is out all night long.

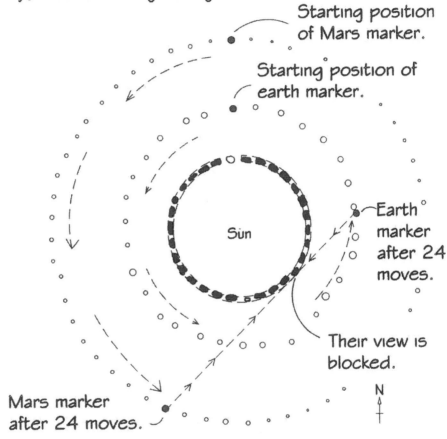

Starting position of Mars marker.

Starting position of earth marker.

Sun

Earth marker after 24 moves.

Their view is blocked.

Mars marker after 24 moves.

N

The chart above is an example of this. It begins with Mars and Earth at opposition on May 5, 3018 BCE, both revolving around the sun represented by the center of the site. I imagine the center, like that of fire, having no density and occupying no physical space. The sarsen structure can be thought of as being an obstruction constructed wide enough for which to block the line of sight between each of the planetary markers.

After the markers moved around the structure approximately 24 increments, their sight line became obstructed by the structure. The narrower the structure, the longer they can see each other. The wider the structure, the quicker they became obscured from each another. That is why the size of the structure was important.

In turn, the distance each ring of holes are from the center of the site plays an important part in the visual timing. The ratio provided from their proportional system is uncannily accurate and very useful with regard to predicting the timing of the planets. They had the ability to predict the view of Mars in the night sky within a few weeks.

According to the planetary chart to the right, Mars was predicted to appear in the morning sky before the sun on or about November 26, 3017 BCE. This was due to the fact that the markers leapfrogged in a counterclockwise direction from hole to hole around the structure; returning into view of one another as the planets literally traveled through the solar system. The structure's width predicted the timing of Mars appearing in the morning sky.

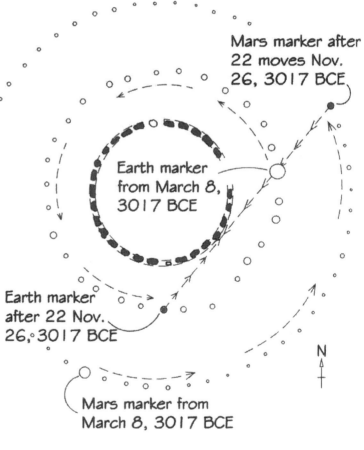

Mars marker after 22 moves Nov. 26, 3017 BCE

Earth marker from March 8, 3017 BCE

Earth marker after 22 Nov. 26, 3017 BCE

Mars marker from March 8, 3017 BCE

N

While studying the proportional step-down ratio, I discovered there is an additional connection between the 194-day line and a 103-day gap. The site taught me that there is approximately 103 days (8 to 9 jumps) prior to an opposition event. The indicator which predicts the 103-day event is forecasted by a 194-day line created between the Earth and Mars markers.

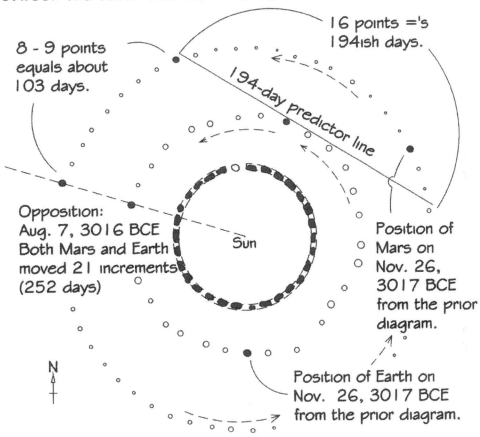

8 - 9 points equals about 103 days.

16 points ='s 194ish days.

194-day predictor line

Opposition: Aug. 7, 3016 BCE Both Mars and Earth moved 21 increments (252 days)

Sun

Position of Mars on Nov. 26, 3017 BCE from the prior diagram.

N

Position of Earth on Nov. 26, 3017 BCE from the prior diagram.

As the planets traveled around the sun, each on their respective course, so did the planetary markers. They were moved from one hole to the next. Eventually the markers lined up with the center of the site predicting the timing of the next planetary opposition. In this realistic example, opposition occurred on August 7, 3016 BCE. The markers leapfrogged 21 increments of time (252 days) from November 26, 3017 BCE.

Setting the clock: Chapter 7

I am indebted to George Zorick for reminding me to investigate setting the planetary celestial clock. From the day of discovery, I have been attempting to determine if the builders of Stonehenge knew earth's place within the galaxy. On earth we can easily determine the four points of the compass rose, but is there a compass rose for earth as it orbits the sun?

The diagram below represents earth's orbit around the sun as it passes the 12 Constellations of the Zodiac. The 'S' on each earth indicates the southern night sky located opposite the sun. As the earth orbits, each constellation eventually becomes south. But, with respect our place in the universe, was it possible to determine what constellation would have been chosen to be considered planetary chart south, a.k.a. galaxy south?

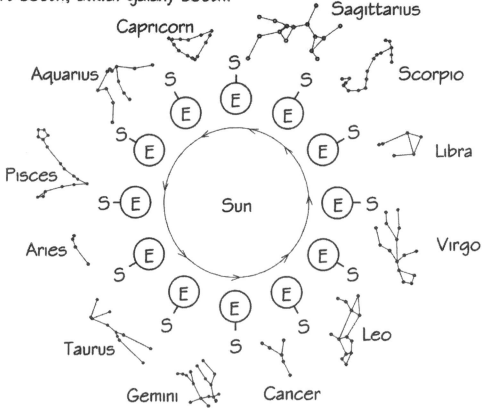

It took me several years to come up with a solution to this question. The answer had to be based on logic and something that they could have determined. I could not ask anyone, I had to determine it for myself. If I could, then so could have they, since I was their student. I can very easily imagine rocks being placed on the inner side of the mounds in the shape of each constellation. The breakthrough moment came with the realization that they would have needed a third element as reference. The element would have been Deneb.

As stated, Deneb is south at midnight on July 17th, along with the constellation of Aquarius. On August 28th, Pisces became south as Aquarius disappeared below the horizon. Deneb maintained its course high above the horizon while circumventing the night sky. On this occasion it is seen at 261 degrees in the west. The pattern of arriving and departing continued for the remaining Zodiac constellations. They appeared above and then disappeared below the horizon, at midnight. Deneb and Cygnus were a continual factor in the onion of Stonehenge. I believe they chose Aquarius as the designated 'site south' or 'galaxy south' constellation. The mental advantage of knowing this would have helped them physically locate earth within the solar system and predict the positions of the Milky Way.

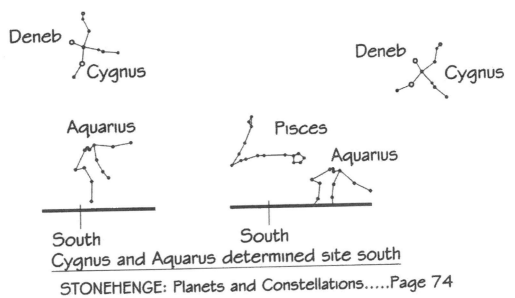

Cygnus and Aquarus determined site south

STONEHENGE: Planets and Constellations.....Page 74

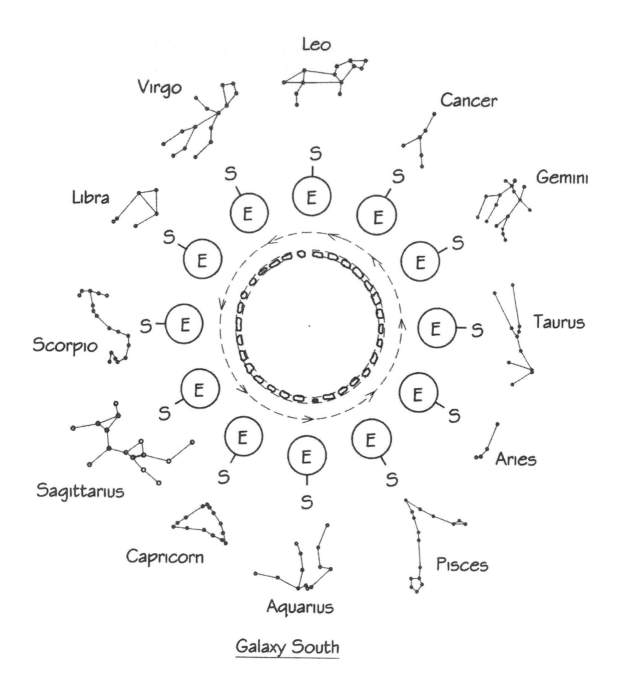

Leo

Virgo

Cancer

Gemini

Libra

S · E

S · E

S · E

Taurus

Scorpio

S · E

E · S

Aries

Sagittarius

S · E

E · S

Pisces

Capricorn

Aquarius

Galaxy South

STONEHENGE: Planets and Constellations.....Page 75

The Sarsen Stones: Chapter 8

The mysterious purpose of the gigantic ring of stones continues as I examine them in elevation. I believe they were constructed a bit differently than popularity would have it look. The two major differences is the design of stones #26 and #11. I believe stone #26 was constructed to be a short stone, no more than a foot above the ground, very much like we see today.

Stone #26

A break in the sequence of stones would have provided an opportunity of visual orientation while occupying the center of the structure. Having been inside the ring, I found it difficult to orient myself to the four cardinal points. Visual cues are extremely helpful for way finding. Both stone #26 and stone #11 would have provided that for the astronomer.

Evidence that supports my claim comes from a photograph I took of the top of stone #27. It is no secret that the builders chiseled raised stone stubs at the tops of the sarsens in order to lock the lintels in place. Doing so, stabilized the structure and helped keep the lintels from sliding off. The top of stone #27 does not have a protruding stub on the side that flanks stone #26. It is however, very pitted and flat.

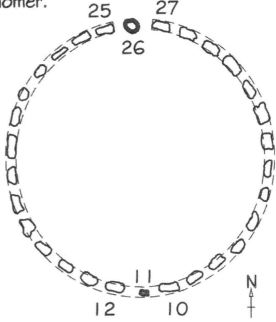

Plan of Stone Ring

Pitted flat top.

Thuban, North Star
in 2687 BCE.*

Top of Stone #27

Also, stone #26 and #11 are the
most northern and southern stones
respectively, in the ring. I argue that
both of them are out of character with
those still standing on site.

I do not believe it is plausible that
stone #26 could be a broken stone,
as other researchers have suggested.
The top measures 6 feet wide and 4
feet thick, 24 square feet of stone. I
am not aware of any other stone
besides #11 and #26, that are said to
be broken and remain in the ground.

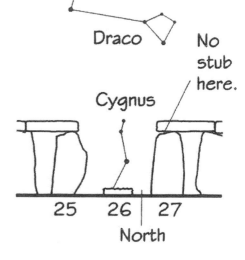

Draco

No
stub
here.

Cygnus

25   26 | 27
North

Stone #26

All others have fallen and left their anchor holes.
Why have the forces of man or nature treated the northern and
southern most stones differently than all the rest? Also, what force
could have sheared this stone so flattly and still have its footing
remain in the ground? Would dynamite? I think not.

On December 25, 2687 BCE,* the wing of Cygnus would have
reached above the horizon and become a vertical visual element
over stone #26. Above that would have been Thuban, the North
Star, located in the constellation of Draco.

*See reference note #2;

Stone #11 marks the southern end of the ring and is about 8 feet tall and 3 feet 5 inches wide. It is hard to find an author that does not show this stone touching the underside of a lintel. I believe stone #80, also known as the 'Altar Stone', was originally a lintel that bridged over stone #11. Doing so, would allow stone #11 to perform its duty as a gnomon and continue the purpose of the lintels.

Supporting evidence to make such a dramatic claim is based on details and measurements of the structure, as well as the shape and measurements of stone #80. Adjacent #11 is stone #10 which remains standing in place. It has a protruding stub only a few inches from the edge facing #11. That told me stone #10 supported a lintel, to or over stone #11.

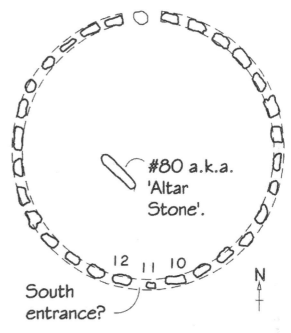

#80 a.k.a. 'Altar Stone'.

South entrance?

12 11 10

N

Stone #12 has fallen and its stub is not clear, but I assume it supported a lintel since that would be consistent with the theme and purpose of the structure. The gap between stone #10 and #11 measures 3 feet 5 inches. The gap between stone #11 and #12 is estimated at 5 feet. The average gap between sarsens that remain standing is approximately 3 feet 6 inches, so I accept 5 feet as being a safe measurement. Also, such a wide gap may have indicated a southern entrance into the structure.

Stone #80 is presently 16 feet 6 inches in length. Over the years it has been chipped away by tourists for souvenirs. It would have been longer in the past, but worst case scenario, I accept its present length in my theory.

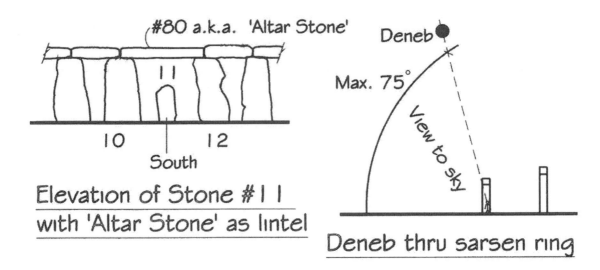

#80 a.k.a. 'Altar Stone'

Deneb •

Max. 75°

View to sky

10   12

South

Elevation of Stone #11
with 'Altar Stone' as lintel

Deneb thru sarsen ring

Adding up all the dimensions, 3'-10" + 3'-5" + 5'-0" = 12'-3". I am comfortable with a 16'-6" lintel spanning a 12'-3" gap. That would have left 26 inches at each end for support. When stone #12 fell, so did lintel #80, and because of its unique color and stone content, it was moved to occupy its present position. In addition, its shape and thickness is consistent with that of other lintels.

The ring of sarsens were capped for the same reason the grand sarsens were capped: To pigeon hole a passing star at midnight. Again, that star was Deneb. A clue to this reasoning came to me as I drew the stones. I noticed, as the stones reached up and met the underside of the lintels, they arched inward forming a niche.

Recognizing the star niche correlation, I created a plan of the structure at the point where the sarsens touched the underside of the lintels. Notice the wider gaps between the stones at the top, compared to those at the base.

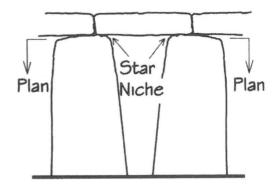

Plan   Star Niche   Plan

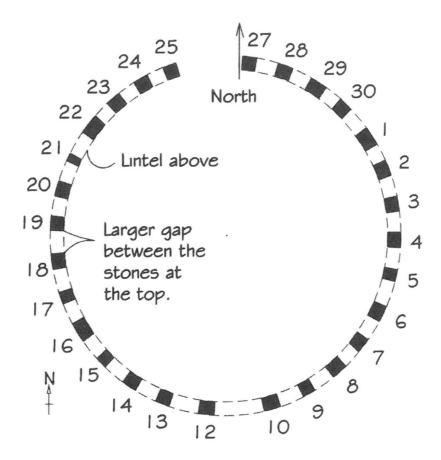

North

Lintel above

Larger gap
between the
stones at
the top.

N

Plan of sarsens just below lintels

Expanding this idea and applying it to the entire sarsen ring, it now became a weekly calendar, in lieu of a monthly one, like that of the grand sarsen structures. Beginning at stone #26 and working clockwise, I plotted their position on the plan, determined their angle from the center, and compared them to the position of Deneb throughout the year.

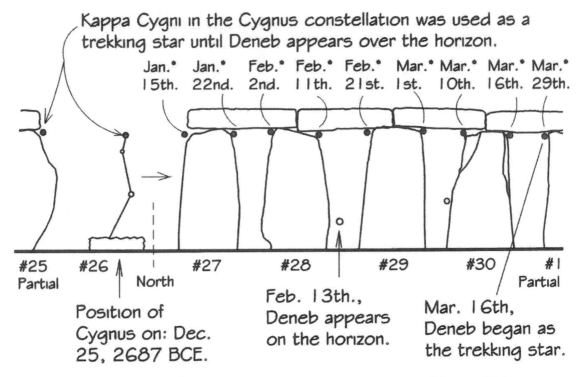

Kappa Cygni in the Cygnus constellation was used as a trekking star until Deneb appears over the horizon.

Jan.* 15th. | Jan.* 22nd. | Feb.* 2nd. | Feb.* 11th. | Feb.* 21st. | Mar.* 1st. | Mar.* 10th. | Mar.* 16th. | Mar.* 29th.

#25 Partial   #26   North   #27   #28   #29   #30   #1 Partial

Position of Cygnus on: Dec. 25, 2687 BCE.

Feb. 13th., Deneb appears on the horizon.

Mar. 16th, Deneb began as the trekking star.

Partial elev. of sarsen ring #25 - #1

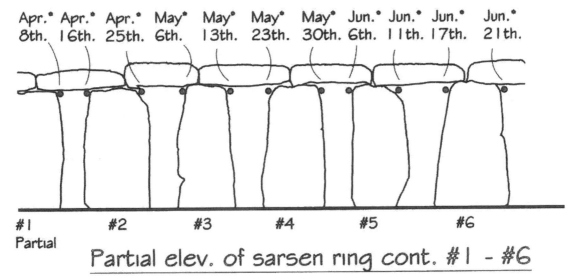

Apr.* 8th. | Apr.* 16th. | Apr.* 25th. | May* 6th. | May* 13th. | May* 23th. | May* 30th. | Jun.* 6th. | Jun.* 11th. | Jun.* 17th. | Jun.* 21th.

#1 Partial   #2   #3   #4   #5   #6

Partial elev. of sarsen ring cont. #1 - #6

*See reference note #82.
**See reference note #15.

STONEHENGE: Planets and Constellations.....Page 81

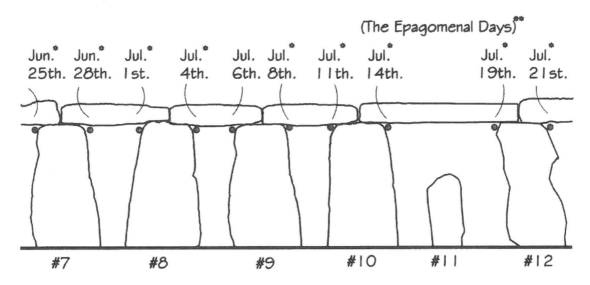

(The Epagomenal Days)**

Jun.* Jun.* Jul.*   Jul.*   Jul. Jul.*   Jul.* Jul.*   Jul.* Jul.*
25th. 28th. 1st.   4th.   6th. 8th.   11th. 14th.   19th. 21st.

#7   #8   #9   #10   #11   #12

Partial elev. of sarsen ring cont. #7 - #12

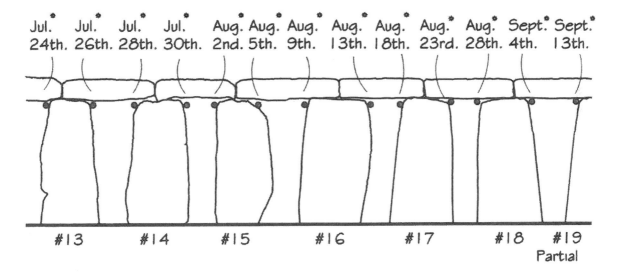

Jul.* Jul.* Jul.* Jul.* Aug.* Aug.* Aug.* Aug.* Aug.* Aug.* Aug.* Sept.* Sept.*
24th. 26th. 28th. 30th. 2nd. 5th. 9th. 13th. 18th. 23rd. 28th. 4th. 13th.

#13   #14   #15   #16   #17   #18   #19
                                                              Partial

Partial elev. of sarsen ring cont. #13 - #19

*See reference note #82.
**See Reference note #15.

Kappa Cygni continues
the trek to stone #26. →

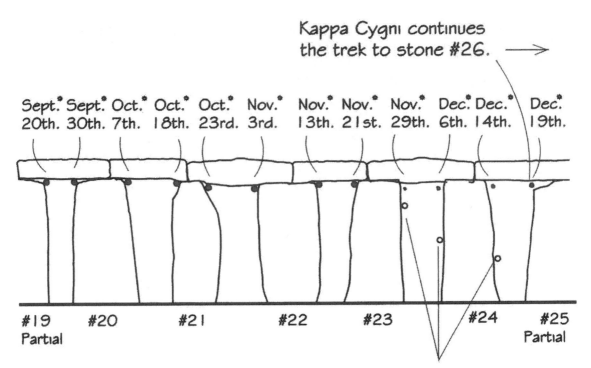

Sept.* Sept.* Oct.* Oct.* Oct.* Nov.* Nov.* Nov.* Nov.* Dec.* Dec.* Dec.*
20th. 30th. 7th. 18th. 23rd. 3rd. 13th. 21st. 29th. 6th. 14th. 19th.

#19   #20   #21   #22   #23   #24   #25
Partial   Partial

Deneb began to acquaint itself with the
horizon as it descended in the evening sky.
The Swan's arm and Kappa Cygni continued
the trek to stone #26.

Partial elev. of sarsen ring cont. #19 - #25

*See reference note #82.
**See Reference note #15.

Sarsen Ring at Midnight: Chapter 9

They were also able to use the ring of sarsen stones to gauge the celestial bodies in order to determine the witching hour, just like that of the 56 cavities.

The diagram shows how the structure could have been used to determine midnight. Once the astronomer saw the sun at dusk and counted the number of stones and gaps past noon, another object would have been tracked in the eastern sky. When that object's position reached the remainder of stones and gaps along the ring, it would have been midnight.

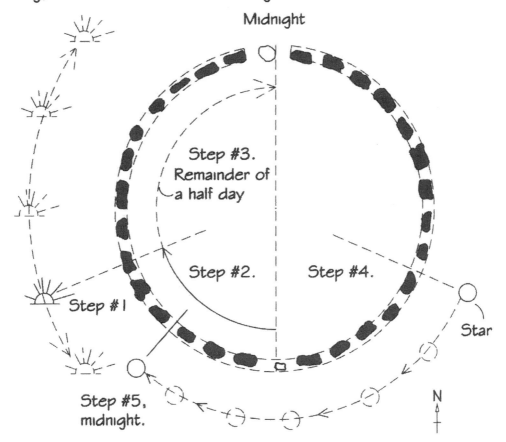

Sarsen ring as the second English clock

Shadows to the center : Chapter 10

While studying stone #11 and trying to determine how it interacted with the site, I discovered that the lintel's shadow above the stone would have reached into the center of the site during the winter solstice. So, the sunshine and shadow passing through the gap between stones #53 and #54 would have created a funny little pie-shaped strike of sunshine on the ground. This could have marked an event for the builders.

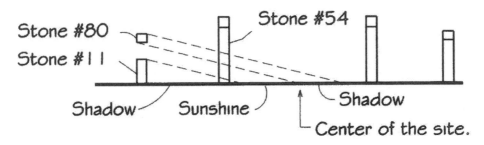

Section through Stone #11.

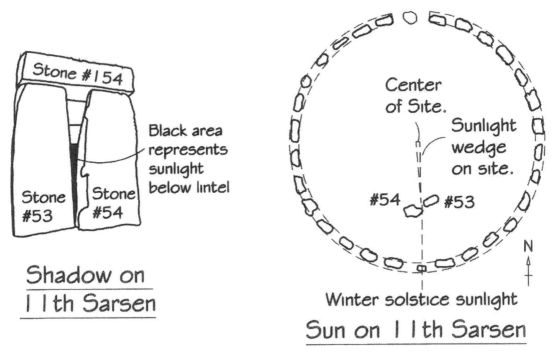

Shadow on 11th Sarsen

Sun on 11th Sarsen

29 Pits of Venus, Jupiter, and Saturn: Chapter 11

I speculate the same proportional system used to locate earth's orbit, also applied to the 'Z Holes'. They are located between the 'Y Holes' and the ring of sarsens. Using the same investigative methods, I believe the builders attempted to identify the distance the 'Z Holes' are from the center, with the planet Venus. Venus is approximately 67.2 million miles from the sun and the 'Z Holes' are about 66 feet from the center of the site; although, they too are constructed with an elliptical orbit.

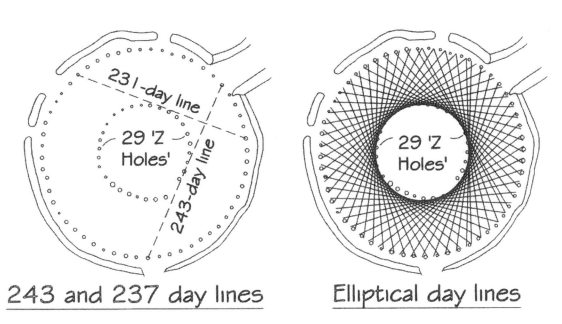

243 and 237 day lines   Elliptical day lines

Venus orbits around the Sun once in about 225 days, which equates to about 18.5 cavities of Mars. At best, a straight line framing in the holes is about 19.5 cavities of Mars, which equates to about 237 days in duration. Interesting is the knowledge that one rotation of Venus lasts about 243 days, and the planet rotates in the opposite direction to the other planets. They could have been interested the duration of its orbit and rotation.

The ring could have also been used for marking the passage of time for other planets. Venus would have needed 19 or 20 holes, while Jupiter would have needed 12, and Saturn 29. It takes just over 12 years for Jupiter and 29.5 years for Saturn, to orbit the sun. Since their orbits are extremely far from the sun, which would have placed their respective planetary markers outside the mound enclosure, I believe they were brought onto the site by multitasking the 'Z Holes'. This would have been convenient with regard to moving the markers and maintaining their correct position.

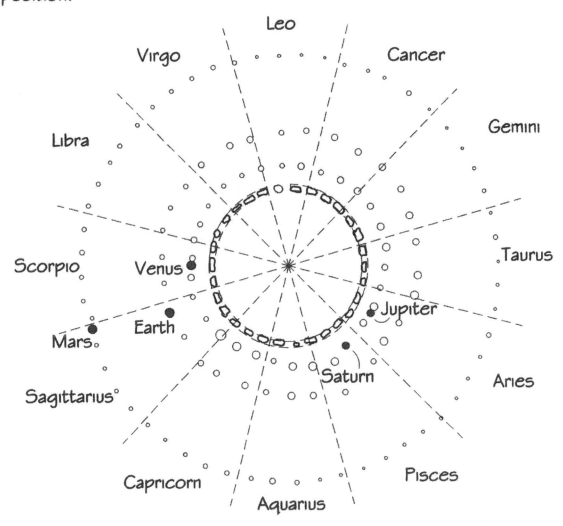

The 'celestial clock' is set for Jan. 14, 2687 BCE.

Cygnus over Amesbury: Chapter 12

Examining the surrounding geometry of Stonehenge, there must have been a profound connection among landmarks in the prehistoric region of Amesbury. The position of Stonehenge is assumed to be at the end of the 'Processional Way'⟨12⟩ leading up from the River Avon. But, that is false. There was also a historic pathway from Stonehenge, which lead southward to the Normanton Downs Barrows. Those barrows were constructed in a row, which gave me the idea to draw a line at their midpoints eastward, in the direction of the river. For curiosity, I then extended the path of the Processional Way southward, across the river. The lines intersected in the middle of a farmer's field.

Looking at the site with new perspective, to me, the line taken from the barrows became an 'imaginary ground line' for the site. If the ancient inhabitants of the area began their ceremonial procession from the point of intersection, and crossed the river from east to west, then that would have been extremely similar to the mythology found in the Egyptian culture. The Egyptians where known to have crossed the River Nile from the land of the living on the east bank, to the land of the dead on the west.

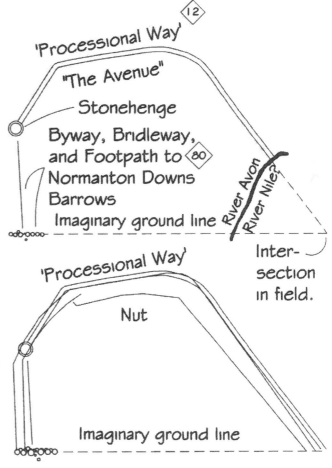

STONEHENGE: Planets and Constellations.....Page 88

After I added the historic footpath from Stonehenge to Normanton Down Barrows and extended the Processional Way across the river, I recognized the figure of the Egyptian God Nut on the landscape. Shown below are sketches depicting the ancient Egyptian goddess.

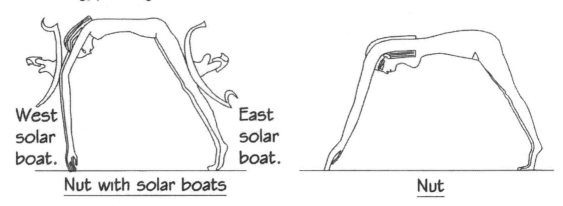

West solar boat.

East solar boat.

Nut with solar boats

Nut

Nut was the goddess of the night sky and depicted the Milky Way; some authors have referred to the Milky Way as the 'river of souls'. So, it is no stretch of the imagination to assume that her aspects would have been incorporated into their religious practices. Discovering the similarites between the shape of Nut and the shape of the Processional Way, demonstrated to me that the builders used the entire site at night, as well as during the day.

Then for fun, I drew a circle from the point of intersection outward to see what would happen. Interestingly, it bisected through both Stonehenge and Woodhenge.

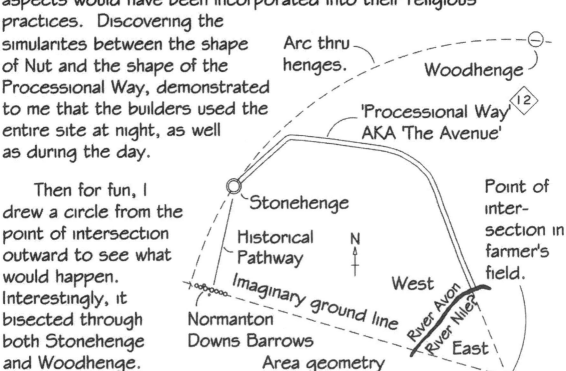

Arc thru henges.

Woodhenge

'Processional Way' AKA 'The Avenue'

12

Stonehenge

Historical Pathway

N

Point of inter-section in farmer's field.

West

Imaginary ground line

Normanton Downs Barrows

River Avon

River Nile?

East

Area geometry

STONEHENGE: Planets and Constellations.....Page 89

Stonehenge now held position at a pivot point between two paths. Continuing my investigation, I wondered if what I found in plan could also be found in elevation, but in this case, the night sky. So, I continued constructing my geometry.

Thinking 3-dimensionally, I imagined myself standing in the farmer's field and on the 'imaginary ground line' at the same time. I drew a line from the point of intersection through Stonehenge creating a 305-degree angle. I called the new line the, 'orientation of the sky'. Theoretically, that made the night sky the Processional Way over head.

My next task was to determine the angle between the 'imaginary ground line' and the 'orientation of the sky' line. Stonehenge was set at about 21 degrees from the 'imaginary ground line', theoretically making it 21 degrees above the horizon. I then asked myself if there were any stars at that location on any particular night.

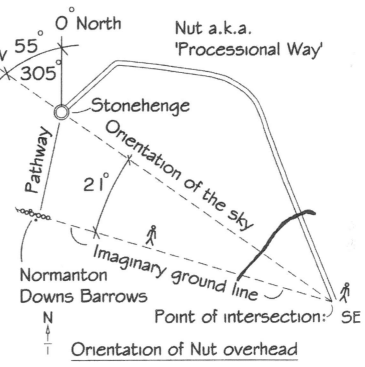

Orientation of Nut overhead

I found that on November 2nd, Deneb was 305 degrees in plan and 18.48 degrees above the horizon.* According to the Egyptian calendar, that was a day of veneration to Hathor.** For me, that made Stonehenge a 'House of Hathor'. But, who was Hathor?

STONEHENGE: Planets and Constellations.....Page 90

"Hathor was one of the most ancient Egyptian goddesses" ⟨62⟩ cults to her go back as far as the Early Dynastic Period of Egypt (3150 - 2686 BCE), ⟨63⟩ which predated the structures at Stonehenge. "She was a popular deity to royalty and common people alike." ⟨63⟩ She was the goddess and personification of many things, including astrology, fertility, motherhood, childbirth, the sky, moon, dance, love, joy, marriage, intoxication, beauty, music, foreign lands, mining, prosperity, protection, and women. She helped the dead journey to the afterlife, and represented the direction west. ⟨79⟩⟨62⟩ Hathor's hair was seen as depicting the omega sign, which was associated with fertility and childbirth. ⟨76⟩

As a goddess she was able to take on the form of a cow and as a woman. But when she became woman, she was described as being seven different women at once. Her many titles included: 'Lady of the universe'; 'Sky-storm'; 'You from the land of silence'; 'You from khemmis'; 'Red-hair'; 'Bright red'; 'Your name flourishes through skill'; 'Lady of the house of jubilation'; 'Mistresses of the west'; 'Mistresses of the east'; 'Ladies of the sacred land', as well as 'in the Book of the Dead'. ⟨66⟩ Her special capacity as a woman was to be present during childbirth, so to pronounce the fate of the child. ⟨66⟩ The sacred animals associated with her included cows, hippopotami, lions, lynxes, snakes, doves, sparrows, swans, vultures, and falcons. ⟨66⟩⟨63⟩ Lastly, Hathor could, in one ⟨79⟩ account, be seen as the pillars on which the sky was supported..." Looking at the structure and seeing the sarsens, to me, I can imagine the structure supporting the sky.

So, what was Egyptian imagery doing here?

Summarizing Gerald Massey from his lengthy book titled, A Book of the Beginnings provides overwhelming evidence that the very early developmental period of the people in the British Isles; their language, rituals, deities, customs, and mythology were strongly influenced by Egyptian culture. Paraphrasing Massey, he described the British adopted mythology of Hathor as, "the golden solar bull of the vernal equinox". She was associated with the rising and setting sun.⟨65⟩ As a goddess, she was recognized with the ability to take the form of a cow and as a woman.⟨65⟩ Being both, associated her with milk; a mother; a wet-nurse to children, and the womb.⟨65⟩ In some areas of Britain, Hathor was associated with the color of white and as a lunar cow.⟨65⟩ The disk between her horns could have very easily been seen as a full moon.⟨65⟩ Taking that concept one step further, could they have perceived the red disk between her horns shown in Egyptian images, as the representation of other celestial objects; such as planets and stars? Especially, red planets and red stars.

Mars has always been identified as being a red planet, and it just so happens Deneb is located directly next to the 'North America Nebula' (NGC 7000)*, which can be seen as being red in photographs. Also, it has been established by astronomers that this nebula is the type in which new stars are produced. It is not known if the early inhabitants knew of its existence, but for me, it reinforces the alluring qualities of birthing symbolism that I have already related to Stonehenge.

Another connection between Hathor and Deneb would have been through the use of bird imagery. As stated above, there were many types of birds associated with Hathor, and one of them was a swan. It is fascinating to me that a star in a constellation having a very early history of having been depicted as a celestial bird, was used by the structure as an instrument for monitoring time.

According to all known accounts, astrology goes back as early as 410 BCE, by the Babylonians⟨64⟩ in the form of cuneiform writing. If all of what I have discovered about Stonehenge is true with regard to tracking planets; Cygnus being used to gauge time; a ratio system used to organize site elements; the structure seen as the personification of Hathor in order to provide newborn

*See reference note #2.

children with their fate, then is Stonehenge the forerunner of astrology? If so, then was information being developed in Britain and then sent to the east, in lieu of what has previously been assumed? That information originated in the east and traveled west. Did astrology originate at Stonehenge?

"Astrology could be described as the study of correspondences between cosmic pattern and human experience. These cosmic patterns are differentiated primarily in three ways: according to the relationships of the various planets (including the Sun and Moon) to one another; according to each planet's relationship to the Earth; and according to the relationship of the planets to the signs of the zodiac." ⟨64⟩

I have demonstrated how the inhabitants were tracking Venus, Mars, Jupiter, and Saturn in relation to Earth, along with their timely opposition. Other researchers have demonstrated how the site and structure was able to track and monitor the movements of the sun and moon. I have also shown how they used the site in order to gauge time. Lastly, I have discussed how they were able to use the constellations to logically discover the orbital cycle of Mars and how they could have chosen Aquarius as the most likely constellation to be 'site south'. Stonehenge, seen as a 'House of Hathor', lead me to conclude that it was used as a place of astrology, long before history accepted or discovered it, in other locations.

Furthering my investigation, I began studying the position of Woodhenge. Per my plans, Woodhenge is 12 degrees clockwise from the point of intersection. I determined that the wing of Cygnus would have stood over the structure on January 23rd.* According to the calendar of festivals, it was the 'Day of Hathor'.** I question whether a long forgotten celestial theme has been discovered.

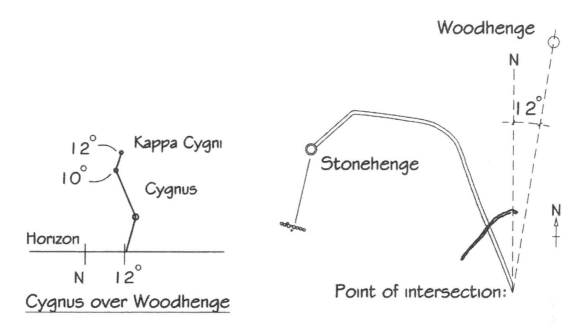

Cygnus over Woodhenge

Woodhenge from point of intersection

On April 1st, Deneb would have been 55 degrees from north,* which indicated another day of celebration to Hathor.** Presently, this location is a grove of trees enclosed by streets in a very populated area of Amesbury. It's wedged between Amesbury Bypass, London Road, and Porton Road. There may be merit to this location being historic because London Road's route curves around the site, possibly to avoid the physical obstacle that may be masked by the trees. Although there is no evidence documented on the Historic Environment Record (HER) of archaeological finds at this site, my research may warrant the need for further investigation.

This position also aligns with the spine of Nut. While standing on the pathway looking east, Deneb would have been over the grove of trees, venerating a day to Hathor. But, looking west on September 17th, Deneb would have been 275 degrees around

*See reference note #2.
**See reference note #15.

from North, which would have indicated the beginning of the month of Hathor and a festival dedicated to that celebration. This discovery may give new insight into how and when the path may have been used.

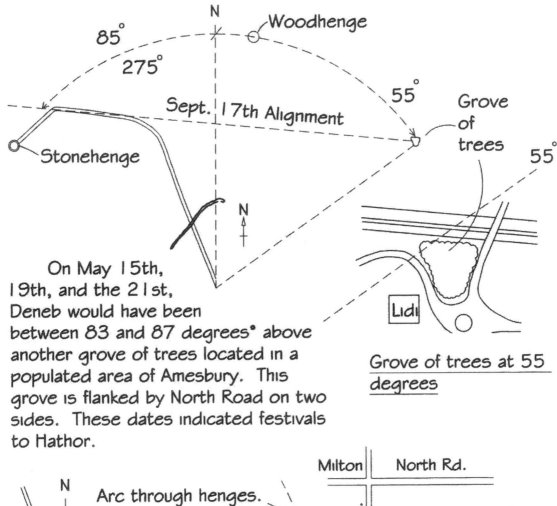

On May 15th, 19th, and the 21st, Deneb would have been between 83 and 87 degrees* above another grove of trees located in a populated area of Amesbury. This grove is flanked by North Road on two sides. These dates indicated festivals to Hathor.

Grove of trees at 55 degrees

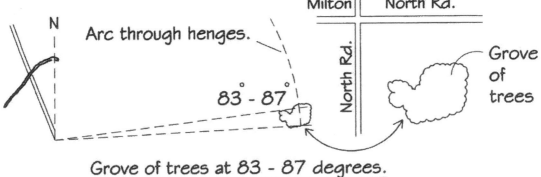

Grove of trees at 83 - 87 degrees.

*See ref. note #2. **See ref. note #15.

STONEHENGE: Planets and Constellations.....Page 95

On August 26th, 27th, and 29th, Deneb would have been over the Wilsford Group Barrows between 256 and 259 degrees*. According to the calendar of festivals** they would have been the days to celebrate the 'Day of Jubilation in the heart of Rae', a birthday of Nut, and a birthday to Heather, respectively.

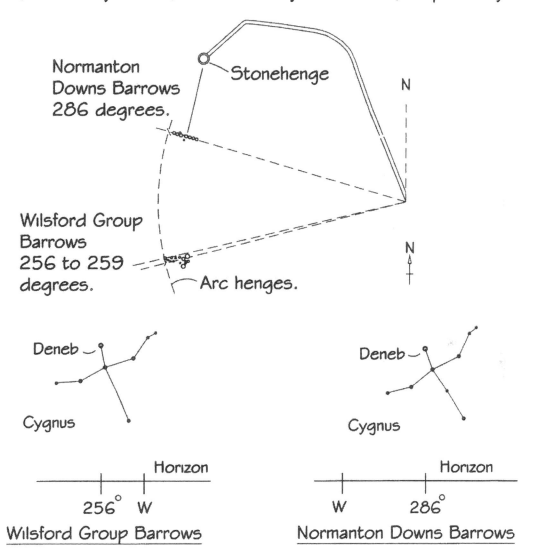

On October 4th, Deneb would have been over the Normanton Downs Barrows at 286 degrees*. According to the Egyptian festival calendar it would have been the 'Festival of Hathor'.

*See ref. note #2.   **See ref. note #15.

From the center of Stonehenge, Deneb would have been 47 degrees northeast on March 21st,* which indicated the 'Festival of the restructuring of the Heavens' and the 'Coming forth of the Great Ones from the House of Ra'.** This alignment coincided with the angle of the Processional Way leading to and away from Stonehenge.

On December 23rd, Deneb would have been about 340 degrees,* which indicated a feast day for the celebration to Hathor.** The alignment coincided with the angle of the Processional Way and the point of intersection in the farmer's field.

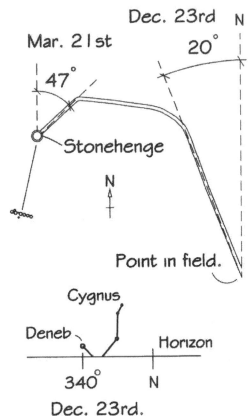

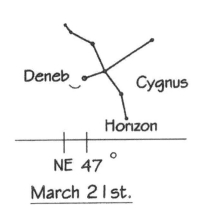

March 21st.

Dec. 23rd.

From the center of Stonehenge, Deneb would have been able to be seen over several of the structures located at Woodhenge on the dates of April 14th, 15th, 16th, and April 21st.* These dates indicated a week long celebration the following respective events: 'Celebrations in the House of Ra and Heru' (Horus); 'Festivals of Heru and Bast'; 'Holiday of Ra and his Shemsu' (followers); 'Feast of Wadjet'.**

*See reference note #2.
**See reference note #15.

Likewise, the inhabitants would have been able to see Deneb in the direction of Stonehenge while standing at the Southern Circle ⟨70⟩ and Woodhenge on the dates of August 13th, 14th, 17th, 19th, and 20th,* which indicated the respective days of celebration for the 'Day of battle between Horus and Set'; 'Day of Peace between Horus and Set'; 'Rituals in the Temples of Ra and Horus'; 'Procession of Horus to Neith'; and 'Thoth ordering the healing of the eye of Horus'.**

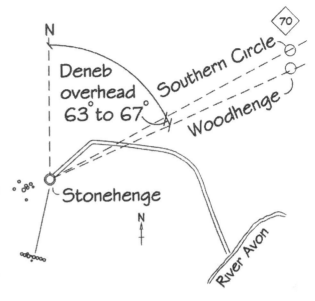

Stonehenge and Woodhenge

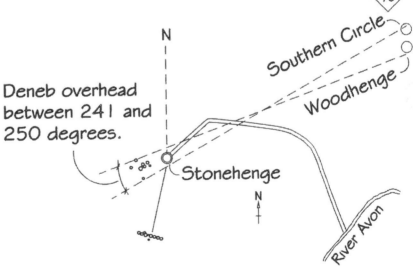

Woodhenge and Stonehenge

*See reference note #2.
**See reference note #15.

In the Egyptian pantheon of god and goddesses, Ra, Horus, and Wadjet were very interconnected. They had many similarities regarding their traits, attributes, symbolism, and common relational associations with other deities. Ra was known as the 'God of the Sun'. He was depicted as a man with the head of a falcon, which included a sun disk encircled by a snake resting on his head.⟨72⟩ Hathor was identified as his consort, recognized at times as his mother, wife, and daughter.⟨79⟩ Humans were believed to be ⟨73⟩ created from his tears and sweat; thus making him a celestial 'cow'. The Eye of Ra was equated with the disk of the sun with a snake wrapped around it.⟨74⟩ The 'Eye' was an extension of his power, but it also behaved as an independent entity, which was personified by other Egyptian gods and goddesses, such as, Wadjet and Hathor.⟨74⟩ At some point during Egyptian mythology, Ra and Horus became so synominous, that the two eventually merged into one entity.⟨69⟩

Before they merged, Horus was one of the most significant ancient Egyptian deities dating as far back as prehistoric Egypt.⟨69⟩ He was known as the 'god of sky and kingship' and was usually depicted as a falcon or a falcon-headed man.⟨67⟩ His consort was Hathor and his right eye was associated with the sun god, Ra.⟨67⟩ His left eye was sometimes associated with the moon.⟨67⟩ The 'Eye of Horus' was known for protection, royal power, good health,⟨67⟩ and seen as a personification of the goddess Wadjet,⟨67⟩ who was depicted as a rearing cobra and appeared as the snake or snakes wrapping around the sun disk.⟨67⟩

The goddess Wadjet was depicted as a snake or cobra and could be seen wrapped around the sun disk.⟨71⟩ She was known as a serpent goddess of justice, time, heaven, and hell.⟨71⟩ Her close association with the sun gave her a reputation as the 'lady of flame'.⟨71⟩ When she was depicted as the mother to Horus, Hathor became his wife, in lieu of his daughter.

For a long time, archaeologists have been looking for a connection between Woodhenge and Stonehenge. I believe the link is in the form of Egyptian symbolism. I have previously stated that Stonehenge was a 'House of Hathor' and I now believe it was one of the 'seven ladies of Hathor'; particularly, 'the lady of the universe'. Since Hathor was so entangled with Horus in Egyptian mythology, numerous star alignments in veneration to Ra and Horus between Woodhenge and Stonehenge, and Cygnus would have been visible over Woodhenge on January 23rd. Woodhenge very possibly could have been known as 'the House of Jubilation', another house of Hathor.

The following song was dedicated to Hathor and I believe could have been a description of Woodhenge:

I built a house for the goddess,
Made of the wood of the sycamore tree.
Under the leaves of the palm tree,
I eat bread in honour of her.
Hathor, Hawk of the Sky,
Rest in the limbs of my tree.
Hathor, House of the Sun,
Live in my house forever. ⟨75⟩

It would be interesting to determine if Sycamore was used to build Woodhenge. Also, I believe there is a direct correlation between Hathor as the 'hawk of the sky' to that of Cygnus being the constellation of the 'Swan'. The line that reads, 'House of the Sun', must have been a direct reference to Ra, Horus, and Wadjet.

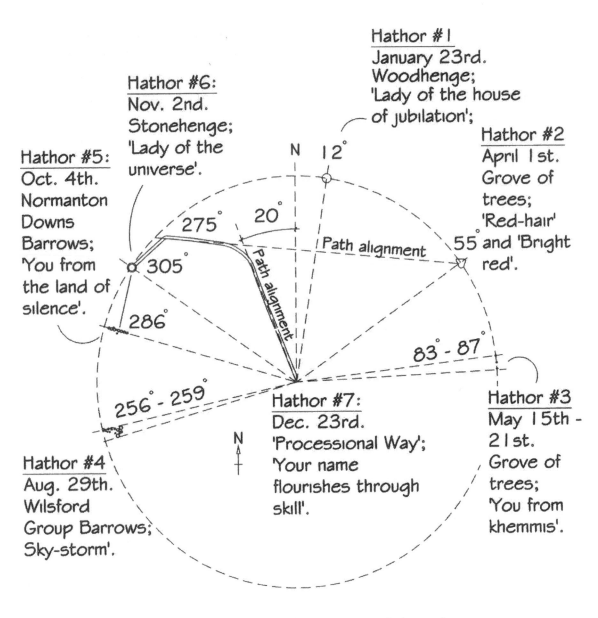

Hathor #1
January 23rd.
Woodhenge;
'Lady of the house
of jubilation';

Hathor #2
April 1st.
Grove of
trees;
'Red-hair'
and 'Bright
red'.

Hathor #6:
Nov. 2nd.
Stonehenge;
'Lady of the
universe'.

Hathor #5:
Oct. 4th.
Normanton
Downs
Barrows;
'You from
the land of
silence'.

N 12°

20°

275°

305°

286°

Path alignment

Path alignment

55°

83° - 87°

256° - 259°

Hathor #7:
Dec. 23rd.
'Processional Way';
'Your name
flourishes through
skill'.

N

Hathor #4
Aug. 29th.
Wilsford
Group Barrows;
Sky-storm'.

Hathor #3
May 15th -
21st.
Grove of
trees;
'You from
khemmis'.

Compulation of 7 Hathors around Amesbury

Note: Several locations need further research and archeological
verification, particularly those located to the east.

The area located in the farmer's field where the intersection occurs, dates to a prehistoric and Roman era. It is designated as a, Field System, East of Normanton. ⟨83⟩ When overlaying Nut onto the Processional Way, the two solar boats riding Nut's body are located at Fighting Cocks to the east and Stonehenge to the west. The eastern boat would have represented the passing of the morning sun and the western boat with that of dusk. Since Stonehenge was used at night, the correlation makes sense.

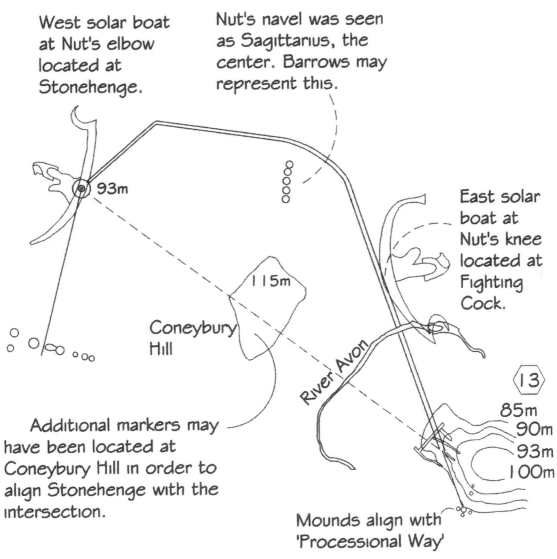

West solar boat at Nut's elbow located at Stonehenge.

Nut's navel was seen as Sagittarius, the center. Barrows may represent this.

East solar boat at Nut's knee located at Fighting Cock.

93m

115m

Coneybury Hill

River Avon

⟨13⟩

85m
90m
93m
100m

Additional markers may have been located at Coneybury Hill in order to align Stonehenge with the intersection.

Mounds align with 'Processional Way'

Area of intersection and solar boats.

I did not intend to discussed sun alignments, which other researchers have proven impact the site, but the alignment I found interesting is its appearance on the horizon on the morning of the summer solstice. The sun appears down the neck of the Processional Way from the northeast onto the site. Taking up the investigation of the alignment myself, I began to plot the degrees the sun appears on the horizon and determined that the sun is approximately 50 degrees from north* on the horizon when it appears on July 13th, the birthday of Ra.**

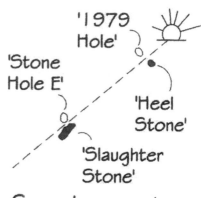

Sun alignment

I suggest that the sun would have appeared between the aligned stones of the 'Heel Stone', 'Slaughter Stone', and neighboring stones as evidenced by their remaining holes, as seen from the center of the site. If all the stones remained and were standing, they would have created a viewing portal for which to watch the event. I can imagine the stones as being synonymous to the horns of the divine cow goddess Hathor, with the sun literally standing as the Uraeus, the symbol of the sun in Egyptian worship.

In addition, "Hathor, along with the goddess Nut, was associated with the Milky Way during the third millennium BCE... and on one account, be seen as the pillars on which the sky was supported..."(79) This quote, provided by Crystalinks.com, has both goddesses associated with the Milky Way and I propose that they worked together. Nut may have represented night and Hathor, day.

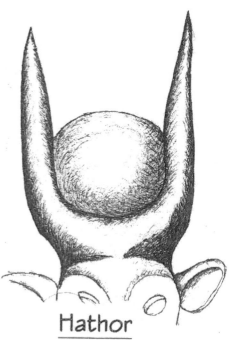

Hathor

The longer I look at the post plan of Woodhenge, the more I want to comment on its meaning and what I think I see in its design. The henge is not circular, but oval. The Uraeus or sun disk within the horns of Hathor is also not round, but a misshapen orb. Likewise, the pupil of the 'Eye of Horus' is not round, but oval. I do not believe the posts were set to mark individual celestial events, but that the entire structure was constructed to represent the sun disk captured in the 'Horns of Hathor'. The center posts take on an oval shape, which could have represented the pupil of the 'Eye of Horus'.

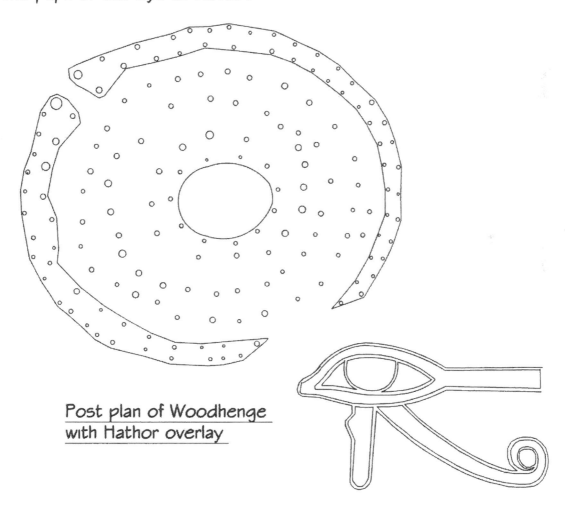

Post plan of Woodhenge
with Hathor overlay

Eye of Horus

Draco: Chapter 13

Early in my evaluation of the Sarsen structure I wondered if the builders revered snakes and snake lore, like that of the Egyptians. Snake fascination has been found all over the world. Was it here also? Taking the constellation of Draco down from the sky and placing it side-by-side on the chalky ground, could have given Stonehenge's architect a concept and a rhythm for design.

Draco side-by-side

Laying a horizontal entablature on Draco's humps is a good start to a schematic elevation.

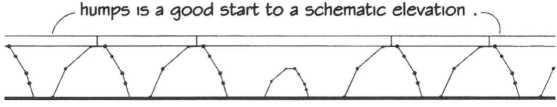

Draco's influence

According to J.E. Cirlot, a closed circle is a symbol of the universe, infinity, or All⟨17⟩ My interpretation of the lintel entablature removes a portion on the north side, thus creating a notch and an imperfect circle symbolizing imperfection, a beginning, and an end, to life and all things.

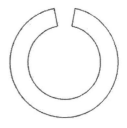

Beginning and an end

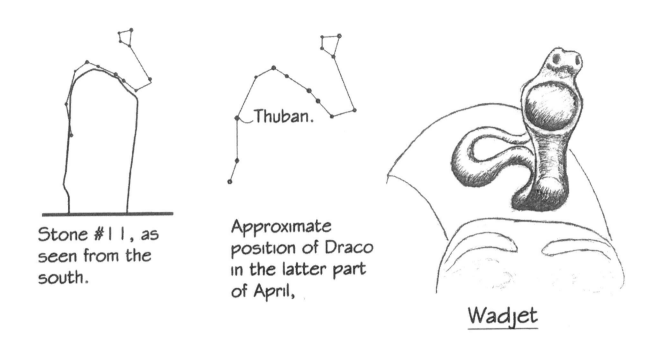

Stone #11, as seen from the south.

Approximate position of Draco in the latter part of April,

Thuban.

Wadjet

The Feast of Wadjet is on April 21st.** The Wadjet is the snake on the headdress of the ancient Egyptian royalty. It adorned their death masks and was a great part of their religious art. It was the protector of kings, the land, women in childbirth, and means, 'The Green One'.[18] I have provided evidence that lintel #80 a.k.a. 'The Altar Stone', could have bridged over stone #11 and that it has the distinct quality of being green. I believe this reinforces my theory for placing a green stone over stone #11.

Wadjet was also strongly associated with the Uraeus, the sun disk; with Fletcher indicating on her website that, "in ancient Egypt the eagle is usually found in connection with the serpent";[19] and with the constellations of Cygnus and Draco providing the site with bird and serpent motif, I propose the strong possibility that Mesopotamian symbolism, iconography, and religion are at work on this site.

**See reference note #15.

Dec. 21, 2012: Chapter 14

During my research to ensure I was the first to discuss the significance of Deneb at Stonehenge, I came upon the writings of Andew Collins, titled The Cygnus Mystery. On his website he states that many cultures, all over the world throughout history, have venerated the constellation of Cygnus. Reading his article sparked a forgotten thought, while studying the areas of the 'teapot' and 'Lagoon Nebula' in Sagittarius, I noticed that on December 21, 2012 the sun appeared at dawn in the area of the 'Lagoon Nebula'. Collins states that the Maya associated the birth of the new sun at the climax of their Long Count calendar on December 12, 2012.[29]

My research places Sagittarius within Stonehenge and the sun at the center. This could mean that one of the structure's purposes was to predict the December 21, 2012 solar occurrence, the same as that of the Maya. Was there shared knowledge? Is this proof that distant people are communicating and moving around from continent to continent over vast oceans, long before Columbus?

Collins proclaims that there are several key megalithic sites in Britain aligned with Deneb, including Avebury; that there is much lore with regard to swans and festivals, such as the, 'Swan-upping' which is associated with a swan feast on St. Swithin's Day, in the middle of July.[30][31] Is this a memory of the birthday to the Egyptian gods, which takes place at the same time using Deneb to mark the calendar? He also makes a connection between Christian traditions associated with St. Martin and geese, and the Celtic New Year known as, 'All Soul's Day', a.k.a. 'The Day of the Dead'.[31]

Gavin White, in his book titled Babylonian Star-lore, writes that, "The Anzu-Bird was envisioned as a gigantic lion-headed eagle, whose enormous wings were thought to create the winds, stir up storms and cover the lands with rolling fog."[61] White equated the ancient constellation to the Greek constellation of Cygnus.

White also writes that, at the base of the Milky Way is found 'Pabilsag', prototype of Sagittarius, whose name means the 'Fore-Father' or 'Chief-Ancestor'. Pabisag's function was to drive discarnated souls from the environs of the earth up into the heavens[23] which made it a guardian and guide for the souls of the deceased.[25] He also writes, "Somewhere in or around Pabilsag is a mysterious astral phenomenon...a 'flash' or 'illumination', and it can be applied to the 'train of a meteor, the 'glitter' of fabric, and even a 'glow' of a person. As a stellar feature...could refer to part of the Milky Way or to one of the many cluster and nebulas found in Pabisag's immediate vicinity".[26] He states the earliest evidence of Pabisag's worship can be dated to the 3rd millennium BCE (3000 BCE).[24]

In Egyptian, Babylonian, and Sumerian star-lore, the personalities the constellations depict, work together to accomplish the rituals of mortals. I found a quote written by White. It discusses the importance of Sagittarius and Cygnus while they worked together during the winter seasons.

> "...with the appearance of the wintertime constellations (Sagittarius, Cygnus, among others) depict the final stages of the stellar calendar. This is the time when the disembodied souls of mankind are spirited away from the environs of the earth and are driven up into the circumpolar regions of heaven to join their ancestors. The constellations in this part of the sky demonstrate that the 'underworld' is not actually located below the earth...but is actually found among the stars. The evidence further indicates that the Milky Way itself was either directly envisioned as the pathway of the dead or that each of its myriad stars was thought to represent a disembodied soul residing in heaven".[23]

There are many more fascinating parallels with Stonehenge to that of Egyptian, Babylonian, and Sumerian lore.

Sumerian & Babylonian influences:
Chapter 15

According to Straw Walker, author of the website, True Ancient History, proclaimed that one of the oldest symbols of man originated in Sumeria, the Omega symbol.⟨32⟩ The Omega symbol is an open ended circle and Walker said it began as a medical devise for cutting the umbilical cord of newborn children.⟨32⟩ He also claimed that it became the symbol for the meaning of life, or the beginning of life, or new life. Ninhursag, the Sumerian god of fertility, was associated with this symbol.⟨32⟩ Likewise, the symbol was also associated with the goddess Hathor, which strengthens my statement that Stonehenge was the 'House of Hathor'.

Stumbling upon this image after I interpreted the lintel entablature was designed with a notch, leads me to believe that this site was used as a medical facility and stone #26 was used as a platform for birthing children. Stone #26 is low to the ground and is large enough to be used as a medical table. In turn, it may also have been used as a fertility altar. Couples may have procreated on the stone in order to better their chances of conception.

Omega symbol
(inverted)

As I go deeper into other important connections between Stonehenge and Sumerian / Babylonian cosmology, I want to impress upon the reader that I only provide my interpretations, connections, similarities, and parallel symbolism of Stonehenge's site features compared to that of the historical descriptions and writings provided by other authors. Please do not hang the messenger if the origin of Stonehenge is different than what you have been lead to believe, for if it walks like a duck, quacks like a duck, looks like a duck, tastes like duck. Duck must be on the menu.

An architect's gift is the ability to manifest words, concept, and symbolism into the built environment. White's diagram of the Babylonian Cosmos helped me make the mental connection between the written descriptions with that of the physical built environment at Stonehenge. I said to myself, "Am I looking at Stonehenge?"

Expanding my research and attempting to follow White's, I obtained several other diagrammatic sources on the subject and read more closely White's text descriptions. Starting on page 35 of White's Babylonian Star-lore, I began making the comparison between the written word describing the Babylonian cosmos and the built environment of Stonehenge.

"Day was born from Night. The Moon and the Sun opened the gates of heaven and flooded the worlds with light[6]".⟨34⟩ "the gods assigned them their fates as the watchmen of Heaven and Earth - their ordained duty to keep the stars of heaven on their predetermined courses...[7]"⟨35⟩ There are some moon and sun alignments connected with this site, of which, I will not go into for fear of digressing. If interested though, please research author and astronomer Gerald S. Hawkins, Stonehenge Decoded: (New York, Doubleday & Company, Inc. 1965).

"The creator-god fashioned a raft...with fertile clay drawn from the watery depths. Thus was the Earth born, a floating island drifting on the face of the Abyss[8]".⟨36⟩ "In due time, the creator fashioned the mountains and marshes, rivers and...mankind and the birds that fill the skies[9]".⟨37⟩ On the broader scope, England is an island, there are creeks and marshes (bogs) in England, the

River Avon is over the eastern hill, and bird lore is abundant on this site. White expands the island theme by suggesting that the Sumerian people used reeds to make floating islands on which to build their houses. That reminds me of the people and structures on Lake Titicaca.

The river imagery is important with regard to human conception, according to White. He indicates that the Sumerians were well aware that semen in a woman's womb produces a birth. White provides a wavy symbol depicting a flowing river, stating that the same sign was used interchangeably for referring to water, son, and semen.[20] Since the River Avon crosses the 'Processional Way', the inhabitants probably used it to access the point of intersection located in the farmer's field as they journeyed from Woodhenge.

According to White, there are 3 levels to the Babylonian concept of heaven dating to the 2nd millennium BCE, "made from different types of stone".[20] "They appear to be constructed as concentric domes or spheres, each dome acting as the ceiling of one level and the floor of the level above[18]".[38] This type of technical language can easily be produced by stacking concentric rings, like that of a typical wedding cake. I believe this is why many of the diagrams I researched have this type of imagery on them. Most of them have a structure depicting a ziggurat or stepped cylindrical pyramid as a structure at the center of the diagram.

"The highest and most remote level of heaven is the abode of Anu, the most ancient god of the celestial realms and father of the earliest gods. Like many other sky-gods he is a rather remote figure having little direct participation in the affairs of ordinary men. His heaven is made from a red stone speckled with patches of black and white.[19] "[39]

Ziggurats or stepped cylindrical pyramids, can be found all over the world. The idea was, the higher off the ground you were, the closer to god you became. I do not believe that concept applies here. What I do believe is that these structures were made to 'be' the heavens, as well as to view the heavens. The grand sarsen structures are of a sandstone material, but I do not know if they have flecks of red, black, or white in them.

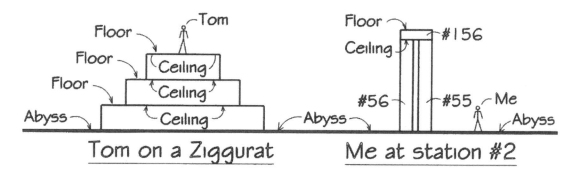

Tom on a Ziggurat   Me at station #2

"The middle realm of heaven was ruled by the king of the gods, usually called Bel or Marduk...the major gods and goddesses of the pantheon were to be found. In this realm, the gods set up a lamp of electrum. It is sometimes thought that this lamp could represent the sun or its daytime light...The middle heaven is made of a dark blue stone.[20] " ◇40

Architecturally, the middle realm of heaven is represented by stones at station #1 and #3. Station #1 has been discovered by me to be an 'opposition portal' for viewing planets and since it faces south, I correlate it with the light of the noon day sun, which casts itself into the center of the site through the portal. The middle realm is the pantheon of the gods, and many religions turn planets into gods. Planets move independently of the constellations, so I believe they would have made special arrangements for them in their heavenly scheme. The planets can be seen in opposition at station #1, but below the lintel.

"The third and lowest heaven is made from a translucent stone; upon it the gods engraved the figures of the constellations. The constellations are best thought of as part of a symbol system by the gods by which they communicate their intentions to mankind.[21] " ◇41

I perceive the lower realm of heaven as represented by station #5 and #4. These two are the first and last stations to see Cygnus throughout the year.

"The color of the stones adds symbolic detail and give some insight into how the whole system was thought to operate. That the lowest heaven...is made from a clear stone presupposes that humanity can see right through it and can therefore observe the...floor of the middle heaven.[22]" ◇[42]

White and other sources he is familiar with, associate the red colour of the highest level of heaven to that of the redness of dawn and dusk. In addition, the white and black colours are speculated to represent, "the darkness of space pierced by the light of the stars".◇[22]

This information gives purpose and validity for the structure, that the gaps between the stones are for viewing the constellations in the night sky. Humanity is supposed to see the constellations "through" the stones. Also, stones at station #2, which I associate with the highest level of heaven, align with the major summer solstice. The sun affronts both sides of these stones, at dawn and then dusk, on this pivotal celestial occurrence.

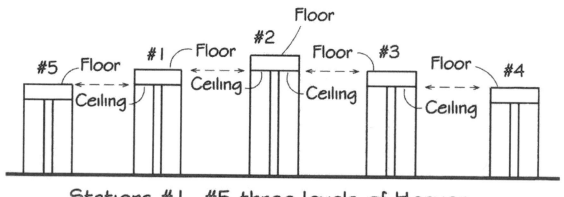

Stations #1 - #5 three levels of Heaven

"Corresponding to the three levels of heaven there were three levels of 'earth'. The 'upper earth' is our familiar world inhabited by mankind. It was conceived as a flat disk floating upon the waters of the Abyss that was surrounded by the boundless salt-water seas.[25]"[43]

"The realm of 'middle earth' lay just below the earth's surface. This realm was envisioned as a vast reservoir of freshwater, called the Abyss, which feeds all the springs, lakes and rivers of upper earth. Middle earth is the abode of Enki, a noble and ingenious god...[26]"[44]

At this point in the environmental symbolism I had to ask myself where 'upper earth' and 'middle earth' occurred and how they were differentiated from each other. The easy answer would be that the structure was the 'upper earth' and the 'middle earth' was the plain of white chalk and anything under ground. But, Enki is said to be an "ingenious god.[26]"[44] So, I got my ingenious thinking cap on and beat White's pages for a viable translation, and came up with my interpretation.

On pages 68 and 69 of White's writings, the 'Anzu-bird' (Cygnus) is considered a "beneficent creature that befriended pious men and rewarded them with a favourable destiny.[5]"[45] "He is a god in animalian form, who inhabited the mountain vastnesses of the east. In the Sumerian poem Lugalbanda, he appears as a cosmological symbol - holding heaven in his hand with the earth set at his feet, while his wings spanned the skies.[6]"[46] "He boasts...and proclaims himself to be 'the prince who decides the destiny of rolling rivers'.[7]"[47] My interpretation of these passages is that the builders used a friendly and helpful god-bird constellation, associated with fertility and water imagery, to link the heavens with the earth.

The stones are anchored in the ground supported by 'middle earth'. Both the 'Anzu-bird' and 'middle earth' are associated with flowing water imagery and I have stated that the builders used Cygnus to gauge their calendar. In short, a god-animal is associated with the stones below the lintels connecting heaven and earth. People need and have a great connection with earth and the land. It is tilled for food and penetrated for fresh water. I do not read that middle earth was seen as a disparaging place, in fact, the two work well together. Our first dwellings may have been caves.

I interpreted 'upper earth' being comprised of the flat lintel disk, floating upon the tops of the 28 sarsens. I interpreted 'middle earth' began from the underside of the lintels down to the deepest hole dug for the structure and mounds. The white layer of chalk symbolized the salty-water of the Abyss; which to me, conveys the imagery of white salt. So thus far, I believe there is a direct physical correlation between the symbolism of Sumerian and Babylonian cosmology with the built environment.

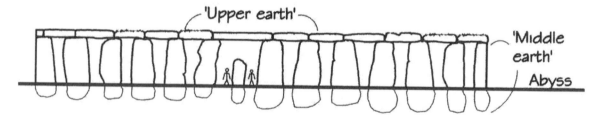

Sarsen ring as upper and middle earth

The similarities of symbolism continue as White discusses the physical terrain of the Mesopotamian homeland, as it relates to Babylonian cosmology.

"A chain of huge mountains bounds the outer limits of the salt-water sea. In their midst lie the gates of heaven, through which the sun and other celestial bodies enter and depart the skies. These mountains are island continents in their own right, probably based on far-distant lands that at various periods had sea-borne trading contacts with Mesopotamia.[32]"[48]

Surrounding Stonehenge's structure is a large flat plain of white chalk. Surrounding and damming that in, was a 5 1/2 foot mound from which to view celestial bodies. If you notice on the plans provided, there are breaks between the mounds in order to access the site, thus breaking the mound 'mountain' symbolism up into individual islands. I imagine the gates of heaven being symbolized by the mounds of the northern and southern barrows. Cygnus a.k.a. 'Anzu-bird' was known as the guardian of the gateway to the dead, and I stated previously that Cygnus, "flew into and nested" at the northern barrow. I also provided a plan with the Milky Way a.k.a. 'river of souls' extending across the site from the northern to the southern barrow, with Crux as its southern anchor. Summing up all of the imagery, Sumerian and Babylonian cosmology fits easily to this site.

The mounds symbolizing, "far distant lands" and "sea-borne trading contacts with Mesopotamia",[48] may very well have been dual symbolism. A representation of the origins of their cosmology, as well as the remembrance of their original homeland. Were the builders of Stonehenge refugees from Sumer, Babylon, or Egypt? Or, could they have come west from, dare I write it, Atlantis?

White also has several passages related to the interaction between Mars and Saturn, which I feel may be a reason that Saturn was brought onto the chart, and why its position was able to be gauged with that of Mars and Earth. "If the Star Cluster reaches the Destroyer: in this year there will be famine.[14]"[49] "If the Star Cluster (Mars) reaches the Serpent (Saturn...): business will diminish.[8]"[50]

Pharaphrasing White, he states that Saturn was known as the, "Destroyer", "the Serpent", and implies that it was strongly related with aspects of death.[51] He also states that, "on entitlement stones" the staff of Zababa, who was known as the, 'king of battles', was frequently set beside the lion-headed staff of Nergal.[52][53][55] Nergal was the, 'god of plague and Lord of the Underworld'.[56] He further states that, "In astrological terms, this could be described as the pairing of Saturn and Mars, two of the most baleful planets",⟨53⟩ and that Mars was identified with Nergal.⟨54⟩

Having Saturn, Mars, and Earth on the site allowed the builders to know when they were in close proximity to each other in the sky. Remember, the orbits of the planets are not perfectly flat to the sun and each other. I think of their orbits as looking like cat whiskers and the nose as the sun. During some transits, the plantes would look as if they may collide by passing behind one another, while at other times, they are very much apart. Depending on where each planet is on its trek around the sun will affect its elevation above the horizon. I imagine when Saturn and Mars appeared to collide in the sky, the people of Stonehenge needed to beware of the benevolent forces of the, "Destroyer"⟨49⟩ (Saturn) and the planet associated with war, Mars.

Mars was not seen as all bad, per White's comments, "red, bright or white objects are nearly always treated as favourable signs".⟨56⟩ Mars has been known as a red planet for a very long time.

Digging deeper into the Sumerian and Babylonian religion I came across Inanna, who was their god of love, beauty, sex, desire, fertility, war, combat, and political power.⟨57⟩ She was the god who could descend into the underworld and return.⟨57⟩ Her description is a lot like Hathor's, but Inanna had a major war aspect associated with her personality. White writes, "Inanna's lust for war and carnage is frequently praised in Sumerian literature. Many of her warlike attributes are recorded in the Sumerian poem Inanna and the Mountain of Ebih, which recounts the goddess' destruction of a mountain realm that refused to submit to her will. The poem praises her as the 'lady of battle'..."⟨81⟩

What I found to be very interesting was her star symbol. It was an eight pointed star with several concentric rings at the center. On first glance it looks like a star could, but I think it has a deeper meaning. She is associated with the planet Venus. With that knowledge, I wondered if the symbol was proportional to site elements found at Stonehenge. After reconstructing the symbol from pictures and then overlaying it on the site. I found that the intersections of the wedges coincided with the hole locations of Venus. Also, the location of the points coincided with the positions of Mars. Its proportions are that of Stonehenge.

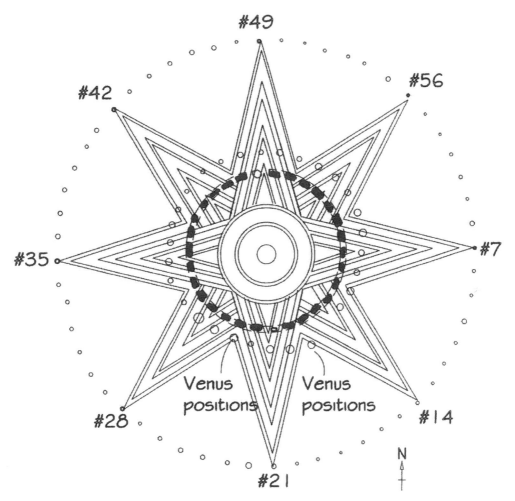

Inanna overlaid on Stonehenge

This symbol has been interpreted by other researchers to only represent Venus. I believe Stonehege is evidence that it simultaneously represented Mars. Taking a harder look, the middle of the star has two concentric circles, not just one. Four of the wedges are prone to the cardinal directions, but the other four are set at a diagonal and underneath the first. This symbol probably represented the overlay of two distinct planets, each maintaining its own identity, one for Venus and the other for Mars.

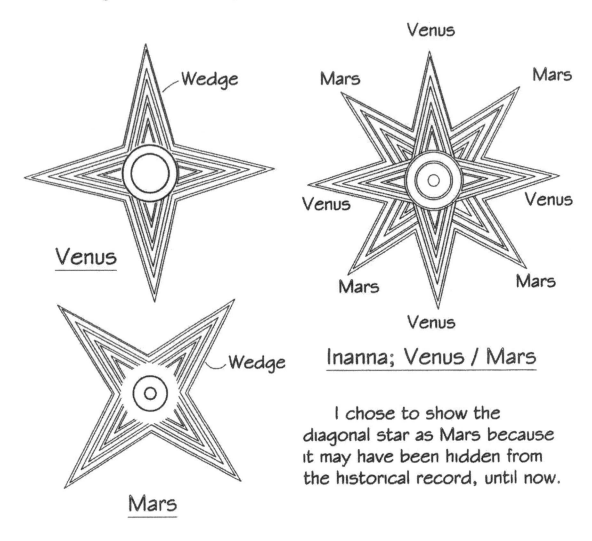

Venus

Wedge

Mars

Venus

Inanna; Venus / Mars

I chose to show the diagonal star as Mars because it may have been hidden from the historical record, until now.

Inanna was sculpted as a bird-woman holding the symbol of a rod and ring in each hand. All the gods held the symbol and it was presented as an offering to kings. The ring is not a complete circle and the rod was usually shown at a diagonal to the ring. In the Early Dynastic Period of Egypt, it was found to be held in the talons of a bird to honor Horus. It represented eternal protection and became the cartouche encircling the names of their kings.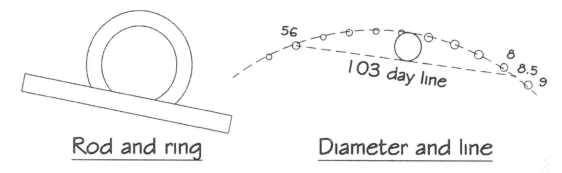⟨58⟩

I present and compare this symbol because I think it looks strickenly similar to the 'diameter and line' geometry produced by the step-down proportional ratio system used on site.

56

103 day line

8
8.5
9

Rod and ring   Diameter and line

As an architect, I find it intriguing to discover the direct use of a symbol in a structure. The four superimposed golf tee looking symbol shown below, is Sumerian cuneiform writting for the word 'heaven' or 'sky'. I found it to be the same shape as the portal slots between the stones, which were used to view the stars and heavens.

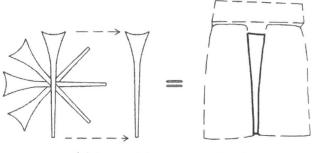

=

AN = Heaven / sky

The final evidence of Sumerian / Babylonian influence and cosmology on Stonehenge are the etched ax heads found on several of the sarsens. I have seen the carvings and they depict original bronze age tools.   There is historic evidence that the Sumerians invented the ability to smelt, cast, and shape bronze tools.

I believe there is a direct physical correlation between the symbolism of the Sumerian, and then later, Babylonian Cosmology to that of the built environment of Stonehenge.

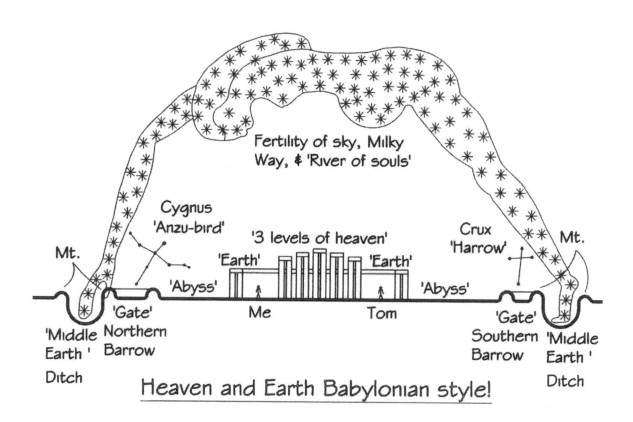

Heaven and Earth Babylonian style!

Stonehenge today: Chapter 16

Asked simply, "Can Stonehenge still be used today? Yes, even though its not completed. Cygnus and Deneb remain above the horizon all year-round. The difficulty is during the summer months, when Deneb reaches about 84 degrees in altitude. It can still be seen while standing behind the structure, but it would be hard on the neck. Presumably, the construction of Stonehenge was built to mark the days on the Egyptian calendar. The use of Deneb can memorialize any date a modern-day builder of a stonehenge finds important.

The diagrams below show the dates in which Deneb can be seen through the gaps between the stones. If those dates mean something to the reader, then you have an additional connection to Stonehenge.

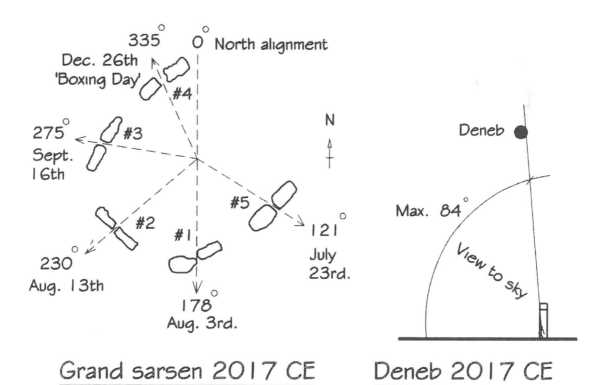

Grand sarsen 2017 CE   Deneb 2017 CE

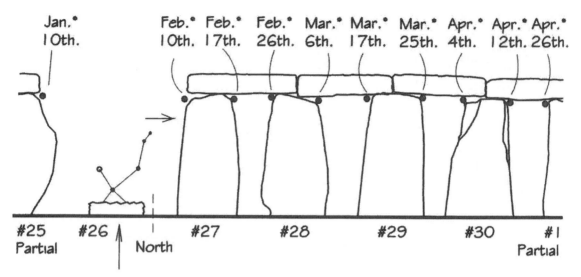

Jan.* | Feb.* | Feb.* | Feb.* | Mar.* | Mar.* | Mar.* | Apr.* | Apr.* | Apr.*
10th. | 10th. | 17th. | 26th. | 6th. | 17th. | 25th. | 4th. | 12th. | 26th.

#25
Partial

#26

North

#27

#28

#29

#30

#1
Partial

Position of Cygnus on:
Jan. 22, 2017 CE.*

Partial elev. of sarsen ring #25 - #1

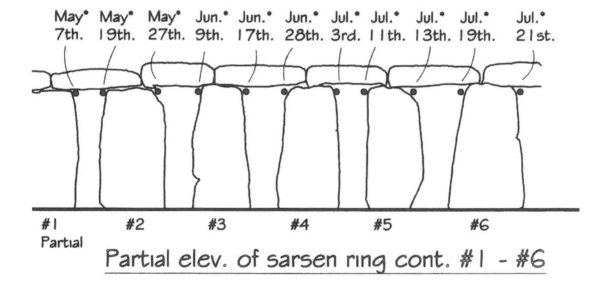

May* | May* | May* | Jun.* | Jun.* | Jun.* | Jul.* | Jul.* | Jul.* | Jul.* | Jul.*
7th. | 19th. | 27th. | 9th. | 17th. | 28th. | 3rd. | 11th. | 13th. | 19th. | 21st.

#1
Partial

#2

#3

#4

#5

#6

Partial elev. of sarsen ring cont. #1 - #6

*See reference note #82.
**See reference note #15.

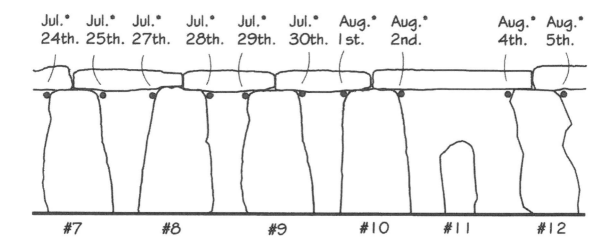

Jul.* Jul.* Jul.*   Jul.*   Jul.*   Jul.*   Aug.*   Aug.*   Aug.* Aug.*
24th. 25th. 27th.   28th.   29th.   30th.   1st.   2nd.   4th. 5th.

#7   #8   #9   #10   #11   #12

Partial elev. of sarsen ring cont. #7 - #12

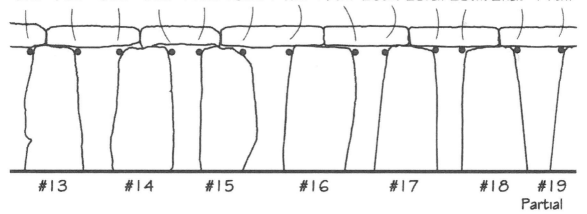

Aug.* Aug.* Aug.* Aug.* Aug.* Aug.* Aug.* Aug.* Aug.* Aug.* Aug.* Sept.* Sept.*
6th. 7th. 8th. 9th. 11th. 13th. 14th. 17th. 20th. 23rd. 28th. 2nd. 11th.

#13   #14   #15   #16   #17   #18   #19
                                                                        Partial

Partial elev. of sarsen ring cont. #13 - #19

*See reference note #82.
**See Reference note #15.

STONEHENGE: Planets and Constellations.....Page 124

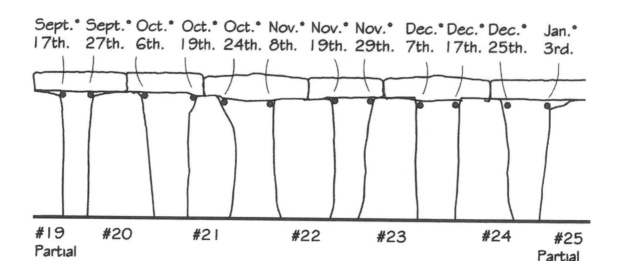

Sept.° Sept.° Oct.° Oct.° Oct.° Nov.° Nov.° Nov.° Dec.° Dec.° Dec.° Jan.°
17th. 27th. 6th. 19th. 24th. 8th. 19th. 29th. 7th. 17th. 25th. 3rd.

#19   #20   #21   #22   #23   #24   #25
Partial   Partial

Partial elev. of sarsen ring cont. #19 - #25

Intervention?: Chapter 17

I believe everything I have stated is true, but I ask myself, "Is there more to their story". Knowing everything I know now, I believe there is enough information on this site to enable a launch window to Mars and Venus. Could Amesbury be a 5,000 year-old Cape Canaveral? I do not say this lightly and over the years, the more I discovered, the stronger my thinking regarding this question became.

Straw Walker discussed a physician named Lulu who may have fled the Sumerian city of Ur, prior to its capture by Sargon's armies. Walker questioned whether Lulu obtained one of the Chariots of the Gods to make his escape.⟨32⟩ I understand the reign of Sargon may have been during the era of sarsen construction, so his conquest of the city may coincide with stone construction. The game of time is found to be flexible with regard to the dating of Stonehenge.

°See reference note #82. °°See Reference note #15.

But frankly, even before reading Walker's writing, I wondered if the mile long Cursus north of Stonehenge, could have been a runway for that type of vehicle. Could Lulu have taken important members of society with him and made England their refugee home; landing on a 700 year-old runway?

The Cursus

o⁻ Stonehenge

Lulu's runway?

The length and width is exactly the same as a modern day air strip. The elevation change is approximately 52 feet. Each end is at 107 meters and the middle dips to 91. The change in elevation of 15 meters or 52 feet over half a mile, which is less than a 2 percent slope. In architectural terms, the Cursus is flat.

Is there evidence in the soil of the Cursus, such as engine exhaust, higher levels of radiation, special ions, atoms, or space aged chemicals to determine if it was used as a landing strip for a spacecraft?

In Remembrance:

This section memorializes friends and family that have departed. Like those buried at Stonehenge, these pages will be edited to include those that will pass. Each person will be associated with the orbit of Mars at the time of their passing. For this first edition, I honor the life of Codi Joyce and George Zorick. Remarks have been provided by their family member.

Codi Preston Joyce: 1991 to 9/27/2015; Mars position of #50: Codi is remebered by his loving father, John Joyce. The following are in his words: "Taken too young, loved by many, and forgotten by none. You did not go alone, for part of us went with you. You will always be in our hearts until we meet again!"

"Codi was murdered at a house party in Munhall, PA. The family continues to fight for justice, despite knowing since day one the names of the individuals that participated in his senseless murder. Not a single arrest has been made - for any crime, this despite a ruling of a homicide and despite Codi being brutally choked and beaten to death. This despite multiple witnesses, despite individuals failing to render assistance, despite individuals leaving a murder scene and despite a confessional text obtained. Where is the justice? Do the Allegheny county authorities go by the laws of the state of Pennsylvania or do they have their own...? Please explain!"

"We all miss him deeply! Codi loved his sports and had a passion for music. He was very handsome and had an infectious smile. He could light up the room with his jokes and laughter. He was never afraid to roll up his sleeves and help out a relative, a friend, a friend's parents, or anyone who asked. He was kind and had a soft heart. He was the mentor for his younger brother and sister... He was the cousin everyone wanted to hang out with... He was our Son! We love you Codi Preston Joyce!"

As a friend to John Joyce and onlooker into the death of Codi, I have many questions concerning the conduct and procedures of the investigating authorities. No one has been charged for any crime, not assault or even under age drinking. I am asking someone with investigative legal experience and impartiality to review the evidence and history of the case. After several year, I understand the case remains open. An important factor of the case may be: That one or more members of the investigative authority may be blood relatives of those who killed Codi. Could it boil down to a simple act of sweeping the case, and those involved, under the rug?

George D. Zorick: 1969 to Sept. 1, 2017; Mars position of: #52. George is remebered by his loving sister Angie Z. Gregory words: "George died at the young age of 48. He was a loving son, brother, father, and grandfather. He never knew a stranger and was always there to help anyone in need".

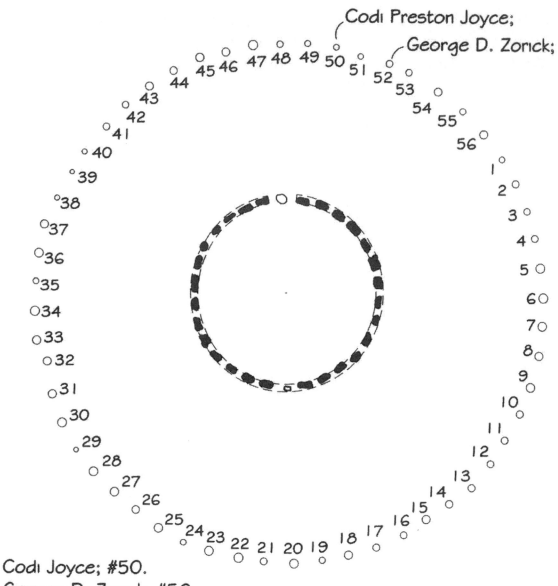

Codi Preston Joyce;

George D. Zorick;

Codi Joyce; #50.
George D. Zorick; #52

STONEHENGE: Planets and Constellations.....Page 129

Serpent Mound: Rider One

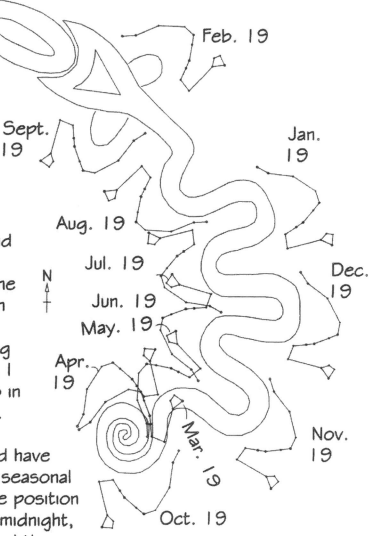

Feb. 19

Sept. 19

Jan. 19

Aug. 19

Jul. 19

Dec. 19

N

Jun. 19

May. 19

Apr. 19

Nov. 19

Mar. 19

Oct. 19

Draco's clock

The Serpent Mound and Stonehenge have been dated to the same time period, so Thuban was the north star during that time. Using Starry Night software, I set the clock of Draco in the sky to 3000 BCE.

I believe they could have used the mounds as a seasonal clock, representing the position of Draco in the sky at midnight, to that of the shape and the orientaion of the serpent's humps on site.

While researching Ra, Wadjet, and Horus, I came across an image of the 'Eye of Horus' in a way I had not seen before. It was shown as a line sketch and it was not complete. I recognized the partial image as the head of the snake at Serpent Mound, located in Ohio. Shocked at the correlation of what I may have discovered and what it may mean historically, the following is my interpretation of the imagery:

Step 1: Original design of the 'Eye of Horus' incorporated a falcon and cobra, which represented a unified Upper and Lower Egypt. Horus' right eye symbolized the sun.

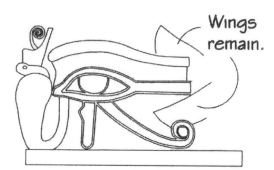

Wings remain.

Step 2: The image becomes flipped; representing the left eye of Horus and the moon. Most of the falcon has been removed, but the wings remain.

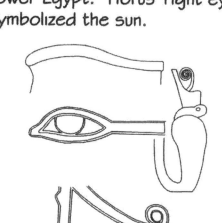

Step 3: The image has been broken apart and the snake flipped to the opposite side of the eye.

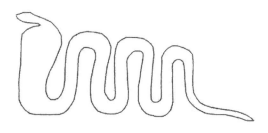

Step 4: An image of the 'Holy Snake', which represented Wadjet from Egyptian art, is added.

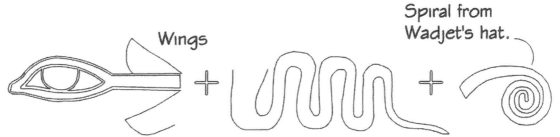

Wings

Spiral from Wadjet's hat.

Step 5: Combining, rotating, and eliminating the imagery.

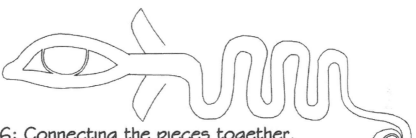

Step 6: Connecting the pieces together.
The eye now looks like the head of a snake.

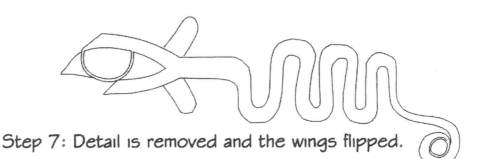

Step 7: Detail is removed and the wings flipped.

Step 8: The head becomes transfigured and
turns were added to the spiral at the tail.

STONEHENGE: Planets and Constellations.....Page R1.3

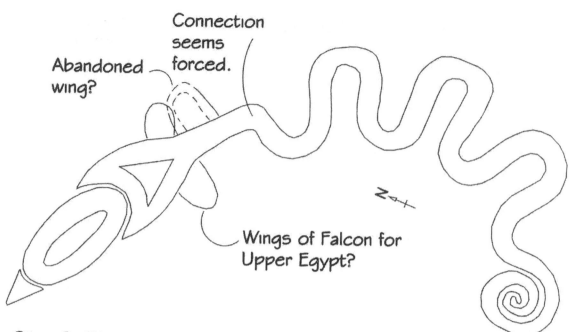

Abandoned wing?

Connection seems forced.

Wings of Falcon for Upper Egypt?

Step 9: Fitting the elements to site constraints and modifying the head and humps to align with celestial events.

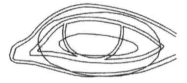

The entire serpent eye is the same size as the entire eye of Horus while the two are at the same proportions or scale.

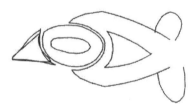

The triangle shaped mound of the 'Serpent' is very similar in shape to that of the corner portion in the 'Eye of Horus'.

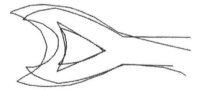

The 'mouth' of the Serpent is actually the outer corner of the 'Eye of Horus'.

The similarities between the symbolism represented in the 'Eye of Horus' and those found in the Serpent Mound go beyond those of characteristics and proportion. The left eye of Horus represented the moon and the right eye the sun. Researchers have correlated the three humps with that of important positions of the moon. Particularly, the moon's maximum south set, minimum north rise, midpoint set, midpoint rise, minimum north set, and the maximum south rise.

Researchers also have stated that the head portion has been aligned with the summer sunset solstice. Likewise, an important aspect of the 'Eye of Horus' is the fact that it was associated with the rising and setting solstices.

I believe there are several reasons that connect the early inhabitants of Ohio to European or Egyptian influences. Russell Burrows has been said to have discovered a cache of Egyptian and European artifacts in a cave located in Illinois. The artifacts are said to have been of very early European history. Also, the depletion of ancient copper mines in Northern Ohio and the Great Lakes Region, have some researchers speculating that the copper may have been sent over to Europe during the Bronze Age. Finally, a structure near Cincinnati, has been described as being similar to England's Woodhenge.

Egyptian Lever: Rider Two

A Hypothesis for the Construction of the Great Pyramid:

Most, if not all construction theories are based on assumption and speculation and are awaiting an opportunity for proof, which often comes with access to the pyramids. The construction hypothesis I present stands on the historical words of Herodotus. Circa 450BC Herodotus wrote the following words describing the construction of the Great Pyramid told to him by priests:

"This is how the pyramid was made: like a set of stairs, which some call battlements and some alter steps. When they had first made this base, they then lifted the remaining stones with levers made of short timbers, lifting them from the ground to the first tier of steps, and, as soon as the stone was raised upon this, it was placed on another lever, which stood on the first tier, and from there it was dragged up to the second tier and on to another lever. As many as there were the tiers, so many were the levers; or it may have been that they transferred the same lever, if they were easily handleable, to each tier in turn, once they had got the stone out of it. I have offered these two different stories of how they did it, for both ways were told me".

Herodotus 485 - 425 BCE; History, 2.125.

While reading his words for the first time I was shocked to find no mention of the use of ropes, wheels, cranes, winches, ramps, pulleys, or levitating devices. It stated that the stones were lifted to the first tier and then 'dragged up' to higher tiers by levers. For something so simple and direct, it is hard to imagine how this is something the Egyptians would not or could not have performed. With ingenuity, deductive reasoning, and the historical account of Herodotus as my creed, I developed my hypothesis and machine.

I propose the machine began with a series of levers all positioned in a straight row up the side of the pyramid. Each tier occupied and structurally supported a base of a lever. The levers were staggered in height in a manner in which each lever was able to pass beneath or above the next. In this case, every other lever was above while every other lever was below. Each timbered lever was set in position and pivoted by a post centered in the middle of the lever. The center post would have been equal distance to each end of the lever, dividing the lever in two equal lengths. While one end rotated and pushed against a block of stone, the other was activated and rotated by a counter weight sliding down the face of the pyramid. The counter-weight could have been on a track in order to make its decent parallel to the levers.

Once the counter weight made contact with a lever, the lever was rotated and force was directed to the opposite end of the timber where a block of stone was dragged up and placed onto the next lever. Each lever was able to rotate 360 degrees in place without interfering with the other levers. A continuing sequence moved a block of stone up the side of the pyramid. The stone block could have been set between parallel guide rails which kept the stone moving in a straight line as it moved up the face of the pyramid.

The counter weight might have been as simple as an empty wooden crate guided by a rail. The workers could have used bags of sand in order to fill the crate with the correct amount of ballast to move the stone up the side of the pyramid. Workers would have stood on each tier of the pyramid, passing the bags to each other in a similar manner as what is known to us as a 'fire brigade'. In order to speed up the relay, several lines of workers could have been utilized at one time.

STONEHENGE: Planets and Constellations.....Page R2.2

As each stone ascended up the side of the pyramid, it would have been accompanied by a counter-weight crate, probably set on top of the stone, allowing the stones and crates to move together up the face of the pyramid. This would have saved a lot of time and energy The only ropes necessary would have been used as safety lines for the workers standing on the narrow tiers of the pyramid.

In order for the counter weight to make a controlled descent down the face of the pyramid, workers could have been positioned along the guide rails with smaller leversThese would have been used as 'friction stops' in order to slow down or stop the momentum of the counter weight. Workers would also be able to stop the stone in position as it moved up the face of the pyramid by the use of 'stop-pins'. This would have given the workers greater flexibility with regard to setting the previous lever in place so to drag the following stone.

While using the above method of 'dragging' the stones, the system of levers can be reset to receive a new stone after the previous stone reaches the third (3rd) lever. The critical path of time is not devoted to moving the stone from one lever to the next , but the time it would have taken the brigade to pass approximately one hundred and fifty - 40 pound bags of sand up the side of the pyramid. If it took 2 seconds to pass a bag between each worker, then it would have taken a total5of minutes to fill a crate with enough sand bags to equal 6,000 pounds with the use of one brigade.

With the use of 4 brigades, the time would be reduced to 1 minute 15 seconds. Thereforeone machine could move a block of stone from one lever to the next every 75 seconds. If a new block of stone could be placed on the machine when the previous reaches every third lever, then a block of stone could be moved and placed every 3 minutes 45 seconds. With the placement of 4 machines, one at the middle of each side of the pyramid, a block of stone could be moved and placed every 3 minutes 45 seconds. With the placement of 4 machines, one at the middle of each side of the pyramid, a block of stone could be moved and set every 60 seconds. This breaks down to about 500 stones set per 8 hour work day, 175,200 per year. It has been estimated that the total number of stone set was 2,500,000, each weighing about 2.5 tons. Given these assumptions, it would take about 14 years to construct the pyramid using 4 machines.

In order to set the final 2 or 3 tiers of stone and especially the apex stone, I estimate that two machines, one on opposite sides of the pyramid, went all the way to the top. I propose the use of 12 machines in the beginning stages of the construction. After a certain number of tiers, the quantity of machines would have been reduced. The wood and materials would have been dismantled and reused to extend the machines that remained operational. The final 2 tiers may have been solid stone units since the working area becomes extremely limited at the upper most tiers of the pyramid. Based on the construction technique above, the pyramid could have been built in 5 years.

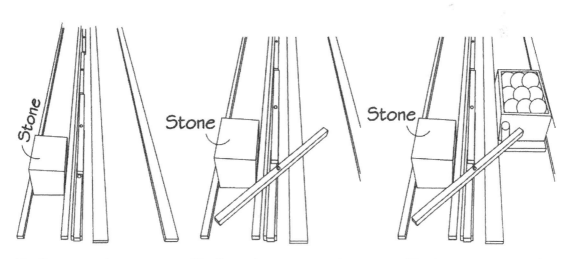

1). Stone in first levered position.

2). First lever moved into place behind stone.

3). A counter weight contacting first lever.

4). A counter weight dragging stone to 2nd lever.

5). A counter weight making contact with 2nd lever.

6). A counter weight dragging stone to 3rd lever. Another stone is set in place.

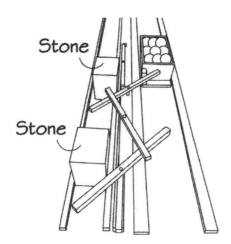

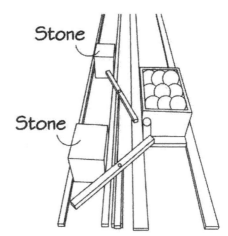

7). A counter weight making contact with 3rd lever. The 1st lever is moved into position waiting to receive counter-weight.

8). A counter weight drags stone and making contact with the 1st lever.

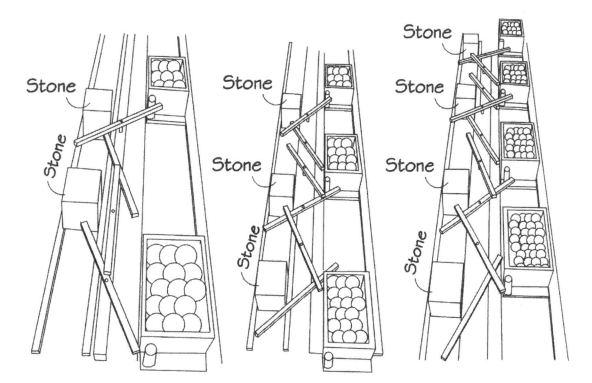

Stone

Stone

Stone

Stone

Stone

Stone

Stone

Stone

9). A counter weight making contact with the 4th lever and another counter weight dragging a stone to the 2nd lever.

10). Counter weights making contact with the 5th and 2nd levers and another stone is being set on first lever.

11). Sequence continues, Counter weights move down dragging stones up to levers.

STONEHENGE: Planets and Constellations.....Page R2.6

Giza's Fourth Structure: Rider Three

    I have been researching the Giza pyramids for a long time. A researcher has suggested the Giza complex to be an electrical power source, by flooding the site with water. I provide the following information to support the argument. On the 'Senmut Map', in a tomb that is over 3,500 years old, there is a blocked off star pattern with three raindrop shaped concentric lines drawn around a star.

    My research equated the three concentric raindrop symbols to mean 'water' or 'rain', which lead me to the terms of 'flood' and 'inundation'. Every year the area was flooded by the Nile River. I have seen old maps showing water coming up to a hill or structure located southeast of the three pyramids. I believe the hill or a lost structure, represents the upper left star on the diagram to the right.

51 Orionis

    Expanding upon the well-known theory that the three pyramids on the Giza plateau represent the three stars in the constellation of Orion, I overlaid the star pattern over Orion's constellation and it was a match. The fourth star lands on a star that is not well known. Starry Night Pro software program calls it, '51 Orionis'.* It was however important enough to show up on some historical constellation maps, like that of the star atlas of Bayer ⟨59⟩ and the star atlas of Hevelius. ⟨60⟩

The fourth star coincides with an existing hill, but it may also indicate a lost structure, directly next to the hill. Seen on aerial maps is, what looks to be a walled structure, aligned with the third pyramid.

Edgar Cayce stated that there is a relationship between the historical archives of the Atlantians and the right paw of the Sphinx. Some have come to suggest and look for a passage from the paw in search of the archives. But, I think his words may be simply a directional location of a structure overlooked on the plateau.

Great Pyramid

I believe the heights of the pyramids were determined by mimicking the angle in plan. From a forth structure, the angle may have been able to be observed. If so, then was the fourth structure an observation platform, like that of pyramids in Mexico? This may be the reason the third pyramid is so much smaller than the other two.

*See ref. note #2.

Second Pyramid

Sphinx

Hill or structure next to modern cemetery southeast of Giza complex. 'Khafre'

'Khufu'

Third Pyramid

Temple wall

Alignment

Lost structure?

'Menkaure'

Atlantis: Rider Four

A dream that has been with me since 1997, is a comfort to me. I was a passenger in a plane flying southeast from Boston. After traveling for a time, it turned east, and then dipped in altitude. Looking out the window, I saw a large structure on land that looked as if it was under water for a very long time. Upon waking I discussed it with my mother. She asked if I had heard of a man named Egar Casey. I told her that I had not. She told me about him and said that he spoke of Atlantis being in the Bahamas.

Recounting the dream, the altitude of the plane was low enough to see a great structure. It was rectangular in shape with massive columns on its west side. I estimated their diameter to be between 30 to 40 feet wide. I later learned, a structure known as the 'Temple of Poseidon' is associated with Atlantis. That could have been the structure. As the plane flew east over the site, the structure became the western most element at the end of a long parade of columns aligning a promenade.

After leaving behind the risen land, the plane continued east for a time. It finally landed at the International Airport of the Bahamas. From there I was placed on a boat and journeyed to the risen land, in the direction of due west.

I estimate the time of its rising to be within my present life time, but not before 2040. So, a word to all those who are in search of it, it will be coming to us. I realize this area of ocean floor is extremely deep, so for it to rise and break the surface of the ocean, a traumatic geological event will have to take place and the coasts of many nations will be affected.

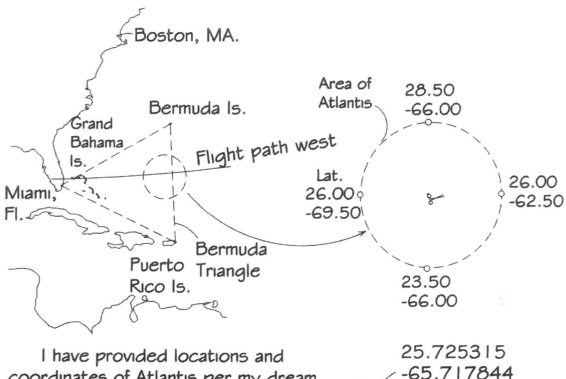

Boston, MA.

Area of
Atlantis

28.50
-66.00

Bermuda Is.

Grand
Bahama
Is.

Flight path west

Lat.
26.00
-69.50

26.00
-62.50

Miami,
Fl.

Bermuda
Triangle

23.50
-66.00

Puerto
Rico Is.

I have provided locations and
coordinates of Atlantis per my dream
information. I researched the area
using satellite imagery and discovered
an interesting anomaly that looks like a
10-mile long analemma at the bottom
of the ocean. There is also a large
mountain just to the north of it that
looks like a mile wide round pyramid. I

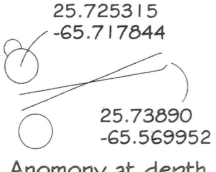

25.725315
-65.717844

25.73890
-65.569952

Anomony at depth

have provided the information as I discovered it. I got the
impression from the dream that the structure of Poseidon used
to be on what is considered the Tropic of Cancer today, the
greatest declination marking the limits of the northern ecliptic.

I believe in the power of dreams. I believe we go home to
God each night while we sleep, because without God's rejuvenating
power, we die. It's like recharging a cell phone battery over night.
A battery can go without a charge for a while, but if it gets too
drained of energy, it loses its life span or dies altogether.

I believe the same goes for humans. Once, while in architecture school, I only received 12 hours of sleep in 7 days. From that experience, I damaged my ability to lose sleep. My bell curve for being able to stay awake and not get extremely depressed, has dramatically changed.

Another reason I take stock in dreams is the time when my friend, Mr. Adams and I, both had the exact same dream. We went over to a friend's house and his mother answered the door. Before that moment, we had never met her. While she talked I could not take my eyes off her huge ugly ring. When we got to the sidewalk, we told each other about having the identical De'ja' Vu moment that focused on her ring. It was spooky and weird.

If, at some point in human history people left Atlantis for a safer place to live, where would they have gone?   In all directions I would think. I believe moving to the opposite hemisphere would have been a safe place to travel. Did Atlantians visit Europe and share their teachings with the local inhabitants? Was their knowledge and religious beliefs delivered to Stonehenge and then to Sumer, Babylon, or Egypt? Was their religion the religion of the Atlantians? Is that why I have found a connection between Stonehenge and Sumer? Is this why construction techniques are extremely similar all over the world? Could Christopher Columbus have re-engineered the escape of the Atlantians?

I tell my kids that there are no bad questions, only bad answers.

Reference Numbers and Research Credit: ◇

◇1 Julian Richards, Stonehenge: English Heritage Guidebooks (London: English Heritage, 2010) Page 6.

◇2 Starry Night Pro: Simulation Curriculum; Simulation Curriculum Corp.; All references to star and planet positions, including dates and times, have been performed using this software. Important dates and times have been crosschecked for accuracy using Cybersky 5 version 5.1.1.0 astronomy software produced by Stephen Michael Schimpf.

◇3 Marilyn Stokstad, David Cateforis, Stephen Addiss, Chu-Tsing Li, Marylin M. Rhie, and Christopher D. Roy; Art History: (Ney York: Prentice Hall, Inc., and Harry N. Abrams, Inc., 2002) Page 68.

◇4 Julian Richards, Stonehenge: English Heritage Guidebooks (London: English Heritage, 2010) Page 31.

◇5 Harriet Crawford, Sumer and the Sumerians: (Cambridge University Press 2004)

◇6 R.J.C Atkinson, Stonehenge: (London: Penguin Group, 1990) Page 27.

◇7 R.J.C Atkinson, Stonehenge: (London: Penguin Group, 1990) Page 28.

◇8 R.J.C Atkinson, Stonehenge: (London: Penguin Group, 1990) Page 22.

◇9 Donald H. Menzel and Jay M. Pasachoff, A FIELD GUIDE TO THE STARS AND PLANETS: (Boston: Houghton Mifflin Company, 1993) Page 292

◇10 Julian Richards, Stonehenge: English Heritage Guidebooks (London: English Heritage, 2010) Page 34.

◇11 Christopher Chippindale, Stonehenge Complete: (New York: Thames & Hudson Inc., 2012) Page not numbered but assumed page 286.

◇12 R.S. Newall, F.S.A., Stonehenge: Wiltshire (London: Her Majesty's Stationery Office 1955) page 12.

◇13 Allerdale Borough Council, http://www.allerdale.gov.uk/community-and-living/deaths-funerals-and-cremations.aspx. Downloadable documents, "Burial on private land", leaflet_-_burial_on_Private_Land.doc Page 2. Visited site on 1/15/2017.

Reference Numbers and Research Credit cont..:◇

14   Donald H. Menzel and Jay M. Pasachoff, A FIELD GUIDE TO THE STARS AND PLANETS: (Boston: Houghton Mifflin Company, 1993) Page 11

15   Note: I cross referenced several sources to ensure consistency. No one source was specifically used: A Festival Calendar of the Ancient Egyptians, http://www.myhome.org/ egyptcalendar.html, visited site 2016, also see; University College London, festivals in the ancient Egyptian calendar; www.ucl.ac.uk/museums-static/digitalegypt/ ideology/ festivaldates.html, 2003, Visited site in 2017, also see; A Festival Calendar of the Ancient Egyptians, www.anglfire.com/ ealm3/shadowsofegypt/festival.html. Visited site 2016, also see; A Festival Calendar of the Ancient Egyptians, http://www.panhistoria.com /www/ancientegyptianvirtualtemple/ calendar1.html. Visited site in 2017.

16   Donald H. Menzel and Jay M. Pasachoff, A FIELD GUIDE TO THE STARS AND PLANETS: (Boston: Houghton Mifflin Company, 1993) Page 387

17   J.E. Cirlot, A Dictionary of Symbols: (Minela NY, Dover Publishing, Inc. 2002) Page123

18   http://www.crystalinks.com/wadjet.html, Author Ellie Crystal 1995 to 2017, visited site in 2017

19   http://www.ancientegypt.hypermart.net/lostsecrets/ Author Audrey Fletcher 1999, visited site in 2017

20   Gavin White, Babylonian Star-Lore: An illustrated Guide to the Star-lore and Constellations of Ancient Babylonia: (London: Solaria Publications, 2014) Page 36.

21   Gavin White, Babylonian Star-Lore: An illustrated Guide to the Star-lore and Constellations of Ancient Babylonia: (London: Solaria Publications, 2014) Page 38.

22   Gavin White, Babylonian Star-Lore: An illustrated Guide to the Star-lore and Constellations of Ancient Babylonia: (London: Solaria Publications, 2014) Page 37.

23   Gavin White, Babylonian Star-Lore: An illustrated Guide to the Star-lore and Constellations of Ancient Babylonia: (London: Solaria Publications, 2014) Page 54.

Reference Numbers and Research Credit cont.: ◇

24. Gavin White, Babylonian Star-Lore: An illustrated Guide to the Star-lore and Constellations of Ancient Babylonia: (London: Solaria Publications, 2014) Page 204.

25. Gavin White, Babylonian Star-Lore: An illustrated Guide to the Star-lore and Constellations of Ancient Babylonia: (London: Solaria Publications, 2014) Page 207.

26. Gavin White, Babylonian Star-Lore: An illustrated Guide to the Star-lore and Constellations of Ancient Babylonia: (London: Solaria Publications, 2014) Page 209.

27. Gavin White, Babylonian Star-Lore: An illustrated Guide to the Star-lore and Constellations of Ancient Babylonia: (London: Solaria Publications, 2014) Page 67.

28. Gavin White, Babylonian Star-Lore: An illustrated Guide to the Star-lore and Constellations of Ancient Babylonia: (London: Solaria Publications, 2014) Page 211.

29. Andrew Collins, The Cygnus Mystery: Author Andrew Collins from his website http://www.andrewcollins.com/ Chapter V. Maya Cosmogenesis, Date of book publication 2006. Visited web site in 2016 and 2017.

30. Andrew Collins, The Cygnus Mystery: Author Andrew Collins from his website http://www.andrewcollins.com/ Chapter VII. The Winged Serpent. Date of book publication 2006. Visited web site in 2016 and 2017.

31. Andrew Collins, The Cygnus Mystery: Author Andrew Collins from his website http://www.andrewcollins.com/ Chapter IX. The Waters of Life. Date of book publication 2006. Visited site in 2016 and 2017.

32. Straw Walker, The True History of Ancient Civilizations / Sumerians / Akkadians / Egyptians: http://trueancienthistory.blogspot.com /2012/12/ancient-sysmbols.html?m+1 Sunday, 16 December 2012. Visited the site in 2017.

33. J.E. Cirlot, A Dictionary of Symbols: (Minela NY, Dover Publishing, Inc. 2002) Page 204.

Reference Numbers and Research Credit cont.: ◇

34) Gavin White, Babylonian Star-Lore: An illustrated guide to the Star-lore and Constellations of Ancient Babylonia: (London: Solaria Publications, 2014) Page 35, Referencing his, The Babylonian Cosmos section, source #6, to Horowitz 1998, page 144. (Exaltation of Istar, lines 25-27). referencing White's bibliography section, Horowitz 1998. Mesopotamian Cosmic Geography, Eisenbrauns.

35) Gavin White, Babylonian Star-Lore: An illustrated guide to the Star-lore and Constellations of Ancient Babylonia: (London: Solaria Publications, 2014) Page 35, referencing his, The Babylonian Cosmos section, source #7, to Horowitz 1998, page 145. (Exaltation of Istar, lines 29-30). Referencing White's bibliography section, Horowitz 1998. Mesopotamian Cosmic Geography, Eisenbrauns.

36) Gavin White, Babylonian Star-Lore: An illustrated guide to the Star-lore and Constellations of Ancient Babylonia: (London: Solaria Publications, 2014) Page 35, referencing his, The Babylonian Cosmos section, source #8, to Horowitz 1998, page 130 - 131. (Bilingual Creation of the World by Marduk CT 13, 36: lines 17-18). Referencing White's bibliography section, Horowitz 1998. Mesopotamian Cosmic Geography, Eisenbrauns.

37) Gavin White, Babylonian Star-Lore: An illustrated guide to the Star-lore and Constellations of Ancient Babylonia: (London: Solaria Publications, 2014) Page 35, referencing his, The Babylonian Cosmos section, source #9, to Horowitz 1998, page 131. (Bilingual Creation of the World by Marduk CT 13, 37: lines 31 - 32). Referencing White's bibliography section, Horowitz 1998. Mesopotamian Cosmic Geography, Eisenbrauns.

38) Gavin White, Babylonian Star-Lore: An illustrated guide to the Star-lore and Constellations of Ancient Babylonia: (London: Solaria Publications, 2014) Page 36, referencing his, The Babylonian Cosmos section, source #18, to Horowitz 1998, pages 3-19. (KAR 307). Referencing White's bibliography section, Horowitz 1998. Mesopotamian Cosmic Geography, Eisenbrauns.

Reference Numbers and Research Credit cont.: ◇

39 Gavin White, Babylonian Star-Lore: An illustrated guide to the Star-lore and Constellations of Ancient Babylonia: (London: Solaria Publications, 2014) Page 36, referencing his, The Babylonian Cosmos section, source #19, to Horowitz 1998, pages 9-11. Referencing White's bibliography section, Horowitz 1998. Mesopotamian Cosmic Geography, Eisenbrauns.

40 Gavin White, Babylonian Star-Lore: An illustrated guide to the Star-lore and Constellations of Ancient Babylonia: (London: Solaria Publications, 2014) Page 36, referencing his, The Babylonian Cosmos section, source #20 to, Horowitz 1998, page 12. Referencing White's bibliography section, Horowitz 1998. Mesopotamian Cosmic Geography, Eisenbrauns.

41 Gavin White, Babylonian Star-Lore: An illustrated guide to the Star-lore and Constellations of Ancient Babylonia: (London: Solaria Publications, 2014) Pages 36-37, referencing his, The Babylonian Cosmos section, source #21, to Horowitz 1998, page 13-15. Referencing White's bibliography section, Horowitz 1998. Mesopotamian Cosmic Geography, Eisenbrauns.

42 Gavin White, Babylonian Star-Lore: An illustrated guide to the Star-lore and Constellations of Ancient Babylonia: (London: Solaria Publications, 2014) Page 37, referencing his, The Babylonian Cosmos section, source #22, to Horowitz 1998, pages 9 ff. Referencing White's bibliography section, Horowitz 1998. Mesopotamian Cosmic Geography, Eisenbrauns.

43 Gavin White, Babylonian Star-Lore: An illustrated guide to the Star-lore and Constellations of Ancient Babylonia: (London: Solaria Publications, 2014) Page 37, referencing his, The Babylonian Cosmos section, source #25, to Horowitz 1998, pages 16-17. Referencing White's bibliography section, Horowitz 1998. Mesopotamian Cosmic Geography, Eisenbrauns.

44 Gavin White, Babylonian Star-Lore: An illustrated guide to the Star-lore and Constellations of Ancient Babylonia: (London: Solaria Publications, 2014) Page 37, referencing his, The Babylonian Cosmos section, source #26, to Horowitz 1998, pages 17-18. Referencing White's bibliography section, Horowitz 1998. Mesopotamian Cosmic Geography, Eisenbrauns.

◇45◇ Gavin White, Babylonian Star-Lore: An illustrated guide to the Star-lore and Constellations of Ancient Babylonia: (London: Solaria Publications, 2014) Page 68, referencing his, The Babylonian Cosmos section, source #5, to Leick 1991, pages 9-10. Referencing White's bibliography section, Leick 1991. A Dictionary of Ancient Near Eastern Mythology. Routledge.

◇46◇ Gavin White, Babylonian Star-Lore: An illustrated guide to the Star-lore and Constellations of Ancient Babylonia: (London: Solaria Publications, 2014) Page 68, referencing his Anzu-Bird section, source #6, to ETCSL: Lugalbanda & the Anzu-bird, lines111-131. Referencing White's bibliography section, ETCSL - The Electronic Text Corpus of Sumerian Literature, website run by the Oriental Institute of Oxford University.

◇47◇ Gavin White, Babylonian Star-Lore: An illustrated guide to the Star-lore and Constellations of Ancient Babylonia: (London: Solaria Publications, 2014) Page 68, referencing his Anzu-Bird section, source #7, to ETCSL: Lugalbanda & the Anzu-bird, lines 90-110. Referencing White's bibliography section, ETCSL - The Electronic Text Corpus of Sumerian Literature, website run by the Oriental Institute of Oxford University.

◇48◇ Gavin White, Babylonian Star-Lore: An illustrated guide to the Star-lore and Constellations of Ancient Babylonia: (London: Solaria Publications, 2014) Page 39, referencing his, The Babylonian Cosmos section, source #32, to Leick 1991, pages 30-33. Referencing White's bibliography section, Leick 1991. A Dictionary of Ancient Near Eastern Mythology. Routledge.

◇49◇ Gavin White, Babylonian Star-Lore: An illustrated guide to the Star-lore and Constellations of Ancient Babylonia: (London: Solaria Publications, 2014) Page 33, referencing his, Astrology & Ominous Signs section, source #14, SAA8 report 491, lines r 3-4. Referencing White's bibliography section, SAA8 = Hunger 1992. astrological reports to Assyrian Kings. University of Helsinki Press.

Reference Numbers and Research Credit cont.: ◇

50. Gavin White, Babylonian Star-Lore: An illustrated guide to the Star-lore and Constellations of Ancient Babylonia: (London: Solaria Publications, 2014) Page 239, referencing his, Serpent section, source #8, BPO3, page 147, omen 13. for the planetary identifications see Gossmann 1950, section 279 IV B 13 (page 111-112). Referencing White's bibliography section, BPO3 = Reiner &Pingree 1998. Babylonian Planetary Omens part 3. Styx.

51. Gavin White, Babylonian Star-Lore: An illustrated guide to the Star-lore and Constellations of Ancient Babylonia: (London: Solaria Publications, 2014) Page 305, referencing his, Serpent section, source #10, See Textual Sources under Prayer to the Gods of the Night. Referencing White's page 386 referencing X, The text of the poem can be found in B. Foster's Distant Days, myths, tales, and poetry of Ancient Mesopotamia, 1995.

52. Gavin White, Babylonian Star-Lore: An illustrated guide to the Star-lore and Constellations of Ancient Babylonia: (London: Solaria Publications, 2014) Page 304, referencing his, Zababa section, source #2, Hinke 1907, page 57. Referencing White's bibliography section, Hinke 1907. A new Boundary Stone of Nebuchadrezzer I. University of Pennsylvania.

53. Gavin White, Babylonian Star-Lore: An illustrated guide to the Star-lore and Constellations of Ancient Babylonia: (London: Solaria Publications, 2014) Page 305

54. Gavin White, Babylonian Star-Lore: An illustrated guide to the Star-lore and Constellations of Ancient Babylonia: (London: Solaria Publications, 2014) Page 299

55. Gavin White, Babylonian Star-Lore: An illustrated guide to the Star-lore and Constellations of Ancient Babylonia: (London: Solaria Publications, 2014) Page 304

56. Gavin White, Babylonian Star-Lore: An illustrated guide to the Star-lore and Constellations of Ancient Babylonia: (London: Solaria Publications, 2014) Page 32.

57. https://en.m.wikipedia.org/wiki/inanna

58. https://en.m.wikipedia.org/wiki/shen_ring

Reference Numbers and Research Credit cont.:◇

⟨59⟩ Donald H. Menzel and Jay M. Pasachoff, A FIELD GUIDE TO THE STARS AND PLANETS: (Boston: Houghton Mifflin Company, 1993) Page 16, Fig. 5.

⟨60⟩ Donald H. Menzel and Jay M. Pasachoff, A FIELD GUIDE TO THE STARS AND PLANETS: (Boston: Houghton Mifflin Company, 1993) Page 26, Fig. 9.

⟨61⟩ Gavin White, Babylonian Star-Lore: An illustrated Guide to the Star-lore and Constellations of Ancient Babylonia: (London: Solaria Publications, 2014) Page 67, referencing his Anzu-Bird section, source #1, to Black & Green 1992. Gods, Demons and Symbols of Ancient Mesopotamia. British Museum Press.

⟨62⟩ https://www.musesrealm.net/deities/hathor.html. visted site on March 22, 2017

⟨63⟩ https://en.m.wikipedia.org/wiki/dendera_temple_complex. Visited site on March 22, 2017

⟨64⟩ Robert Powel, The Zodiac: a Historical Survey; (Epping, New Hampture: ACS Publications, 1985) Page 2.

⟨65⟩ Gerald Messay, A book of the Beginnings; Originally published 1881.

⟨66⟩ www.hethert.org/seven_hathors.htm copyright 1999-2007 by neferuhethert. Last updated 01/27/10. Visted on Mar. 22, 2017.

⟨67⟩ https://en.m.wikipedia.org/wiki/eye_of_horus

⟨69⟩ https://en.m.wikipedia.org/wiki/horus

⟨70⟩ https://en.m.wikipedia.org/wiki/woodhenge

⟨71⟩ www.crystalink.com/wadjet.html

⟨72⟩ www.crystalink.com/ra.html

⟨73⟩ https://en.m.wikipedia.org/wiki/ra

⟨74⟩ https://en.m.wikipedia.org/wiki/eye_of_ra

⟨75⟩ www.thewhitegoddess.co.uk/the_goddess/hathor_-_eye_of_ra.asp

Reference Numbers and Research Credit cont.: ◇

76 www.gigalresearch.com/uk/hathor-nebheru.php; Text by Antoine Gigal from 2000. Visited site in 2017.

77 Gavin White, Babylonian Star-Lore: An illustrated Guide to the Star-lore and Constellations of Ancient Babylonia: (London: Solaria Publications, 2014) Page 26.

78 Gavin White, Babylonian Star-Lore: An illustrated Guide to the Star-lore and Constellations of Ancient Babylonia: (London: Solaria Publications, 2014) Page 93.

79 http://www.crystalinks.com/hathor.html, Author Ellie Crystal 1995 to 2017, visited site in 2017

80 Julian Richards, Stonehenge: English Heritage Guidebooks (London: English Heritage, 2010) on Key related to dots on area diagram, Page 29.

81 Gavin White, Babylonian Star-Lore: An illustrated Guide to the Star-lore and Constellations of Ancient Babylonia: (London: Solaria Publications, 2014) Page 185.

82 Starry Night Pro: Simulation Curriculum; Simulation Curriculum Corp.; All dates provided from software of star positions have been estimated based on angles taken from center of the site to an estimated reconstruction of structure at assumed niche locations. Dates provided for general overall concept only.

83 Wiltshire Council Monument Full Report 27/09/2017. Archaeology Recorded on the HER to the East of the Stonehenge World Heritage Site. Report generated by HBSMR from exeGesIS SDM ltd. pages 47 and 48.

Graphic Research Credit: ⬡

Covers: Original - Brent Stagnaro. Loosely based on several sources.

⬡1 Original - Brent Stagnaro. Based on several sources - See Andrew J Lawson, Chalkland: an archaiology of Stonehenge and its region (Salisbury: The Hobnob Press, 2007) Page 36, see also; Julian Richards, Stonehenge: English Heritage Guidebooks (London: English Heritage, 2010) Pages 20 to 21 and page 29.

⬡2 Historical stone numbering system; Stonehenge: Plans, descriptions, and Theories; W.M. Flinders Petrie (London: Edward Stanford, 55 Charing Cross, S.W.1880) Page 9, 10, 11, 12. also depicted in Christopher Chippindale, Stonehenge Complete: (New York: Thames & Hudson Inc., 2012) Page not numbered but assumed page 9.

⬡3 Original - Brent Stagnaro. Based on several sources - See Andrew J Lawson, Chalkland: an archaiology of Stonehenge and its region (Salisbury: The Hobnob Press, 2007) Page 36, see also; Julian Richards, Stonehenge: English Heritage Guidebooks (London: English Heritage, 2010) Pages 20 to 21 and page 29, see also; Anthony Johnson, Solving Stonehenge: The New Key to an Ancient Enigma (New York, Thames and Hudson 2008) Page 8.

⬡4 Original - Brent Stagnaro. Based on several previous sources, also see R.J.C Atkinson, Stonehenge: (London: Penguin Group, 1990) Page 28.

⬡5 Original - Brent Stagnaro. Derived to illustrate a concept or idea from the text. Traced from a picture taken while on site.

⬡7 Original - Brent Stagnaro. Based on several sources, also see S.C.I Planet Tracker by: Spherical Concepts, Inc. King of Prussia, PA. copyright 1983 plastic disk; see also Geoffrey Cornelius and Paul Devereux, The Secret Language of the Stars and Planets: (San francisco: Chronicle Books, 1996) Page 21; also see Donald H. Menzel and Jay M. Pasachoff, A FIELD GUIDE TO THE STARS AND PLANETS: (Boston: Houghton Mifflin Company, 1993) Page 386.

Graphic Research Credit: ⬡

⟨8⟩ Original- Brent Stagnaro. Based on several sources - See Andrew J Lawson, Chalkland: an archaiology of Stonehenge and its region (Salisbury: The Hobnob Press, 2007) Page 36, see also; Julian Richards, Stonehenge: English Heritage Guidebooks (London: English Heritage, 2010) Pages 20 to 21 and page 29.

⟨9⟩ Original- Brent Stagnaro. Based on Google satillite images of the ocean floor.

⟨10⟩ Original- Brent Stagnaro. Based on several previous sources - See also Julian Richards, Stonehenge: English Heritage Guidebooks (London: English Heritage, 2010) Page 34; see also Christopher Chippindale, Stonehenge Complete: (New York: Thames & Hudson Inc., 2012) Page not numbered but assumed page 286.

⟨11⟩ Pete Knese, (The Glass Rose), Stain Glass/Lead and Wood, 2016, PK2 Studios, Brooklyn, NY.

⟨12⟩ Original - Brent Stagnaro. Based on a picture of Nut provided in The Secret Language of the Stars and Planets, page 29. Written by Geoffrey Cornelius and Paul Devereux; Their source was from Gods of the Egyptians (vol. 1) by E., Wallis Budge.

⟨13⟩ Original - Brent Stagnaro. Based on an Ordnance Survey map #100049050 produced by the Historic Environment Record (HER). Provided by Wiltshire Council.

Bibliography of Research:

○ Julian Richards, Stonehenge: English Heritage Guidebooks (London: English Heritage, 2010).

○ Starry Night Pro: Simulation Curriculum; Simulation Curriculum Corp.

○ Marilyn Stokstad, David Cateforis, Stephen Addiss, Chu-Tsing Li, Marylin M. Rhie, and Christopher D. Roy; Art History: (Ney York: Prentice Hall, Inc., and Harry N. Abrams, Inc., 2002).

○ Harriet Crawford, Sumer and the Sumerians: (Cambridge University Press 2004).

○ Julian Richards, Stonehenge: English Heritage Guidebooks (London: English Heritage, 2010).

○ R.J.C Atkinson, Stonehenge: (London: Penguin Group, 1990).

○ Donald H. Menzel and Jay M. Pasachoff, A FIELD GUIDE TO THE STARS AND PLANETS: (Boston: Houghton Mifflin Company, 1993).

○ Christopher Chippindale, Stonehenge Complete: (New York: Thames & Hudson Inc., 2012) Page not numbered but assumed page 286.

○ R.S. Newall, F.S.A., Stonehenge: Wiltshire (London: Her Majesty's Stationery Office 1955).

○ Allerdale Borough Council, http://www.allerdale.gov.uk/ community -and-living/deaths-funerals-and-cremations.aspx. Downloadable documents, "Burial on private land", leaflet_-_burial_on_Private_Land.doc

○ W.M. Flinders Petrie, Stonehenge: Plans, Descripton, and Theories. (London: Edward Stanford, 55 Charing Crodd S.W. 1880).

Bibliography of Research:

○ Gavin White, Babylonian Star-Lore: An illustrated Buid to the Star-lore and Constellations of Ancient Babylonia: (London: Solaria Publications, 2014).

○ Edgar Barclay, R.P.E, Stonehenge: Its Earth Works (London: D. Nutt, 270 and 271, Strand 1895).

○ A Festival Calendar of the Ancient Egyptians, ttp://www.myhome.org/egyptcalendar.html also see; UniversityCollege London, festivals in the ancient Egyptian calendar; www.ucl.ac.uk/museums-static/digitalegypt/ideology/ festivaldates.html, 2003 also see; A Festival Calendar of the Ancient Egyptians, www.anglfire.com/ealm3/ shadowsofegypt/festival.html

○ Aubrey Burl, The Stonehenge People: (London Melbourne: J.M. Dent & Sons Ltd, 1987).

○ John Fillwalk, Institue for Digital Intermedia Arts, Ball State University Muncie, IN. (E-mail correspondence).

○ Aubrey Burl, The Stonehenge People: (London Melbourne: J.M. Dent & Sons Ltd, 1987).

○ English Heritage Stone Circle Access, Site visit July 2015.

○ en.m.wikipedia.org/wiki/antikythers _mechanism, Ancient Analog Computer.

○ Science.larouchepac.com/kepler/newastronomy/part 1/ marsyear.html; How long is a Mars year?

○ Julian Richards, Stonehenge: A History in Photographs (Barnes & Noble Publishing, Inc.:2005).

○ John North, Stonehenge: Neolithic Man and the Cosmos: (London: HarperCollins Publisher, 1996).

○ Anthony Johnson, Solving Stonehenge: The New Key to an Ancient Enigma, (New York: Thames & Hudson, 2008).

Bibliography of Research:

○ Gerald S. Hawkins, Stonehenge Decoded: (New York, Doubleday & Company, Inc. 1965).

○ Robert Powell, The Zodiac: A historical Survey: (Epping NH. Astro Computing Services 1985).

○ Harvey & Victoria Bricker, Astronomy in the Maya Codices 2011.

○ Mike Parker Pearson, Researching Stonehenge: Theories Past and Present; (London).

○ J.D. North, Stars, Minds and Fate: Essays in Ancient And Medieval Cosmology; (London and Ronceverte the Hambledon Press).

○ Elizabeth Howell, Stonehenge was and Ancient Burial Ground for the Rich: Study (University College London, April 27, 2013).

○ Colin Roman, The Astronomers:(London, Evans Brothers Limited 1964).

○ Mike Saunders, Stonehenge Planetarium, (Colin Roman, The Astronomers: (London, Evans Brothers Limited 1964).

○ Joan Moore, Stonehenge A Blueprint, (N. Somerset, Joan Moore, 2009).

○ G.E.S. Curtis, An Astronomical Enigma (1998).

○ Fred Hoyle, On Stonehenge: (San Francisco, W.H. Freeman and Company1977).

○ Andrew Collins, The Cygnus Mystery: From Andrew Collins Website 2016 and 2017.

○ Gay Robins, The Art of Ancient Egypt: (Harvard University Press Cambrige, Massachusetts 1997).

○ http://www.ancientegyptonline.co.uk/nut.html (2016).

Bibliography of Research:

- Jaromir Malek, Egypt: 4000 Years Of Art, (London, Phaidon Press Limited 2003).

- Edgar Evans Cayce, Edgar Cayce on Atlantis: (New York, Paperback Library, Inc.).

- Gerlad Messay, A Book of the beginnings: First published 1881.

- Robert Powel, The Zodiac: a Historical Survey; (Epping, New Hampture: ACS Publications, 1985).

- Wiltshire Council: http://www.wiltshire.gov.uk/

- Archaeology Service / Wiltshire & Swindon History Centre.

- Dave Batchelor, Mapping the Stonehenge World Heritage Site. Proceedings of the British Academy, 92, 61-72.

65097634R00093

Made in the USA
Middletown, DE
22 February 2018

You killed my father. Prepare to die.

As you wish.

Inconceivable!

You keep using that word.

I do not think it means what you think it means.

Death cannot stop
true love.

Have fun stormin' da castle!

Rodents of Unusual Size? I don't think they exist.

My way's not very sportsmanlike.

I've got my country's 500th anniversary to plan, my wedding to arrange, my wife to murder, and Guilder to frame for it. I'm swamped!

Let me explain . . . No, there is too much.
Let me sum up.

Buttercup: We'll never survive!

Westley: Nonsense. You're only saying that because no one ever has.

Since the invention of the kiss, there have been five kisses rated the most passionate, the most pure. This one left them all behind. The end.